FOREWORD

Within the framework of the CCET's programme of policy dialogue and assistance to the transition economies, support is provided in the area of privatisation. The first initiative to create an institutional framework for the exchange of relevant information on privatisation took place at the OECD/CCET conference on "Methods of Privatisation of Large Enterprises", hosted by the Polish Ministry of Privatisation, in Pultusk in November 1991. This conference, and subsequent meetings, led to the creation of the OECD/CCET Advisory Group on Privatisation (AGP) in February 1992. Participation is open to the privatisation agencies of all transition economies, member country experts and selected representatives of the private sector and academia.

The AGP provides the framework for a regular exchange of experience between privatisation practitioners in the reforming countries, at the same time enabling them to benefit from privatisation experience in OECD countries. The AGP, which meets twice a year, thus serves as a forum for discussion of important privatisation issues and has created a permanent network of contacts for the exchange of information.

A number of papers presented during the eighth meeting of the AGP (Paris, October 1995) are published in the present volume, on the subject of privatisation of utilities and infrastructure companies. The relevant issues include the need to create an appropriate regulatory framework for natural monopolies prior to privatisation; the techniques for large utility privatisation; an important new area of economic activity, namely the participation of the private sector in infrastructure projects, hitherto regarded as the exclusive domain of public sector investment. The geographical scope is also broad: OECD economies, transition countries and other non-member developing economies that have had extensive experience in many of these areas.

The purpose of this publication is to allow policy makers in transition economies to better understand the advantages and pitfalls of infrastructure privatisation and to learn from mistakes that their counterparts in other countries have made in the past. This is an important prerequisite in order to exploit fully the potential that such strategies offer for the development of a robust private sector and the rapid improvement of the country's infrastructure, without endangering fiscal and budgetary discipline.

The opinions expressed in these papers are solely those of the individual authors and do not necessarily represent the opinions of the OECD or its Member countries. Mr. Stilpon Nestor, Head of Unit, Ms. Karla Brom, Consultant and Mr. Chang Koo Lee, Consultant in the Unit for Privatisation/Private Sector Development of the Directorate for Financial, Fiscal and Enterprise Affairs have prepared this volume and the Introductory Note. This document is published on the responsibility of the Secretary-General of the OECD.

Jean-Pierre Tuveri
Deputy Director of the CCET

OECD PROCEEDINGS

CENTRE FOR CO-OPERATION WITH THE ECONOMIES IN TRANSITION

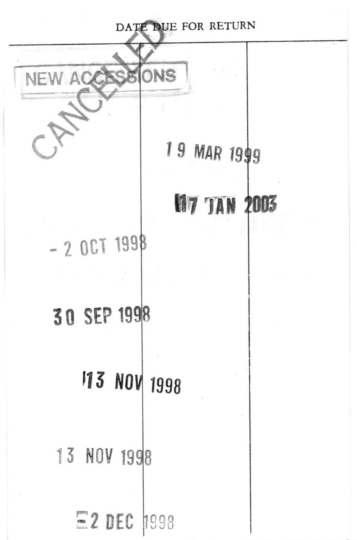
The following texts are published in their original form to permit faster distribution at a lower cost.
The views expressed are those of the authors,
and do not necessarily reflect those the Organisation or of its Member countries.

ORGANISATION FOR ECONOMIC CO-OPERATION AND DEVELOPMENT

ORGANISATION FOR ECONOMIC CO-OPERATION AND DEVELOPMENT

Pursuant to Article 1 of the Convention signed in Paris on 14th December 1960, and which came into force on 30th September 1961, the Organisation for Economic Co-operation and Development (OECD) shall promote policies designed:

- to achieve the highest sustainable economic growth and employment and a rising standard of living in Member countries, while maintaining financial stability, and thus to contribute to the development of the world economy;
- to contribute to sound economic expansion in Member as well as non-member countries in the process of economic development; and
- to contribute to the expansion of world trade on a multilateral, non-discriminatory basis in accordance with international obligations.

The original Member countries of the OECD are Austria, Belgium, Canada, Denmark, France, Germany, Greece, Iceland, Ireland, Italy, Luxembourg, the Netherlands, Norway, Portugal, Spain, Sweden, Switzerland, Turkey, the United Kingdom and the United States. The following countries became Members subsequently through accession at the dates indicated hereafter: Japan (28th April 1964), Finland (28th January 1969), Australia (7th June 1971), New Zealand (29th May 1973), Mexico (18th May 1994), the Czech Republic (21st December 1995), Hungary (7th May 1996), Poland (22nd November 1996) and the Republic of Korea (12th December 1996). The Commission of the European Communities takes part in the work of the OECD (Article 13 of the OECD Convention).

THE CENTRE FOR CO-OPERATION WITH THE ECONOMIES IN TRANSITION

The Centre for Co-operation with the European Economies in Transition (CCEET), which serves as the focal point for co-operation between the OECD and the countries of Central and Eastern Europe, was created in March 1990. In 1991, the activities of the Centre were expanded to include the New Independent States of the former Soviet Union, and subsequently Mongolia (1992) and Vietnam (1995). In 1993, to take account of its broader geographical focus, the Centre was renamed the Centre for Co-operation with the Economies in Transition (CCET).

The Centre operates a number of Special Country Programmes: the Partners in Transition (PIT) Programme, of which the last remaining ''Partner'', the Slovak Republic is negotiating accession to the OECD (the other former ''Partners'' – the Czech Republic, Hungary and Poland – have joined the OECD); the Russian Federation Programme; and the country-specific programmes for Bulgaria, Romania and Slovenia.

TABLE OF CONTENTS

INTRODUCTORY NOTE

The eighth meeting of the OECD/CCET Advisory Group on Privatisation (AGP) took place in Paris on 30 and 31 October 1995, on the subject of "Privatisation of Utilities and Infrastructure: Methods and Constraints". The meeting brought together high-level privatisation officials and policy makers from Albania, Belarus, Bulgaria, the Czech Republic, Estonia, Georgia, Hungary, Kazakhstan, Kyrghyzistan, Latvia, Lithuania, Moldova, Mongolia, Poland, Romania, Russia, Slovenia and Ukraine, experts from international organisations, privatisation officials and other representatives from 17 OECD Member countries and private sector practitioners.

Six papers presented in the meeting are published in the present volume. *Harry Bush*, from the United Kingdom Treasury, discusses issues related to the strategic design of a utilities privatisation programme, drawing on the United Kingdom experience. *Eduardo Bitran* and *Pablo Serra* focus on the regulatory implications of privatising utilities and discuss different options available to policy makers; the Chilean approach constitutes the starting point of their analysis. *John Wilson*, from the New Zealand Treasury, provides a case example of an attempt to allow competition to develop in an industry that remained in state hands. *Adam Ridley* presents an overview of the main issues related to private sector participation in infrastructure projects, with special emphasis on the distribution of risk between the private and public partners. *Douglas Webb* discusses the long-term contractual relationship that develops between the private provider and the state/client, the regulatory environment of this relationship and the availability and scope of guarantee facilities that cover contractual risk. Finally, *Peter Noble,* from the Victoria Treasury in Australia, describes, as a case example, the extensive private sector infrastructure investment programme undertaken in this Australian state during recent years. A number of conclusions can be drawn from these papers and the discussion among AGP participants that ensued.

The decision to privatise utilities and encourage private sector investment in infrastructure projects shares the main objectives of privatisation in general: improving the efficient operation and governance of enterprises and raising money for the state budget. Two other important objectives should be added: freeing infrastructure enterprises from investment constraints imposed by the present-day rigor of public finances; and, most importantly, introducing competition in areas hitherto reserved to state-owned monopolies.

Introducing competition should be the main concern of policy makers in the utility area. The assignment of many of these areas to the public sector in the past reflected concerns with their "natural monopoly" characteristics and the potential for private abuse of monopoly power. Technological progress is contributing to a rapid lowering of entry barriers and thereby is rendering several of these markets contestable. The role of the state should be to facilitate the entrance of third parties that can compete on a level playing field with established, mostly state-owned or privatised, providers of services. Competition/antitrust law enforcement is therefore important in ensuring that no abuse of dominance takes place in the process of opening up the market to new entrants. In cases where direct competition cannot develop due to persistent high economies of scale, benchmark competition, *i.e.* the comparison of prices/output/productivity with other similar operators, might be a useful tool to promote competitive behavior in the industries concerned.

The establishment of an effective regulatory framework will be very important in areas where price competition and direct contestability cannot yet be established. A central concern is the flexibility and adaptability of the price control mechanism. On one hand it should provide incentives to private operators to increase productivity and internal efficiency by allowing them to capture a substantial part of the efficiency gains; on the other, it should protect the interests of consumers by allowing them to benefit from these gains.

An important issue is the institutional profile of the regulator: independent agencies accountable to political authority as opposed to parts of the government apparatus, might meet fewer constraints in developing the considerable amount of expertise needed to effectively address utilities regulation. Specific-industry regulators might have an advantage in terms of flexibility and expertise but might be more vulnerable to becoming captive to the industry's powerful interests. In transition or developing economies, the creation of inter-sectoral regulatory institutions might be a satisfactory answer to the above captivity concerns and, moreover, improve the allocation of scarce human and financial resources available to the public sector.

Pre-privatisation restructuring of utilities industries might be essential for a number of reasons. The most important ones relate to the competition and third party access concerns mentioned above: consumers might greatly benefit by upstream or downstream competition (or, at least, benchmarking) as a result of the breaking up of vertically integrated state-owned monopolies, even when the distribution network is still a non-contestable monopoly. Moreover, restructuring and commercialisation of the industry should result in the clear separation of commercial functions from regulatory ones, assigning the latter to state institutions/regulators. Finally, corporatisation and the establishment of clear commercial performance criteria might give the enterprises in question a chance to prepare for the market place and find leaders that will successfully take them there. However, corporatisation on its own is unlikely to rival the effectiveness of private shareholders in monitoring managerial performance; private ownership is the most effective way to contain rent-seeking behavior by agents, whether they are managers or representatives of the owner/state.

Pre-privatisation restructuring in transition economies is subject to constraints due to the lack of human and financial resources. The answer to these constraints has been in many countries the sale (usually a minority block plus the right to manage) of the vertically-integrated monopolies to strategic foreign buyers capable of restructuring and investing in infrastructure maintenance and development. This might be a good solution where the relevant market is becoming contestable, provided that a regulatory scheme that guarantees third-party access has been put in place(or at least designed) before the sale. If these conditions are not met, the benefits of privatisation might be lost through a decrease in consumer welfare; it is preferable to incur the higher up-front costs of restructuring and ensure the longer term benefits of competitive markets.

Where some minimum level of competition is ensured, transition countries might be well advised to look for strategic investors with enough expertise and financial resources available, instead of relying on narrow local capital markets and scarce domestic managerial resources. In the context of trade sales capital increases can be used as the main tool for privatisation; this will strengthen companies' balance sheets and, if combined with the transfer of control, ensure a healthy start for the privatised company.

In most developed economies, initial public offerings of shares (IPOs) are the preferred method of privatising public utilities. Apart from being the more transparent and politically acceptable method, IPOs also serve other government objectives such as the development of equities markets and the creation of a broad share-owning class. However, a programme based on IPOs requires a coherent and carefully planned privatisation strategy. A major concern is to avoid flooding the market and thereby depressing prices; therefore, some of the larger companies might be privatised in tranches. In the first phases of a privatisation programme pricing policies aim at confidence building among investors and issues are therefore priced rather cheaply. As the programme develops the government's pricing strategy may focus more towards efficient pricing as well as lowering related transaction costs in this area through book building or other similar arrangements.

One of the main goals of privatisation is improving corporate governance. Policy makers should therefore be aware ex ante of the varying governance consequences of different privatisation methods. A strategic investor will, in principle, offer the best post-privatisation governance; however, in this context, minority shareholders should be protected from abuses of managerial power. On the other hand, IPOs, especially when they are combined with restrictive clauses (*i.e.* upper limits on individual ownership of shares, excessive regulatory interference in the event of ownership change or restrictive articles of association that include "poison pills"), may diminish substantially the policing role of the market for corporate control. Weaker monitoring notwithstanding, some of these devices may be necessary to ensure a stable ownership environment at the initial post-privatisation phases. It is important that these initial restrictions have sunset provisions, so that the takeover market may eventually function and the governance environment optimised.

Even if it falls short of outright privatisation, the participation of the private sector in infrastructure projects provides countries with financial and managerial resources to meet their needs for infrastructure maintenance and development and often is a necessity in a period of tight budgetary constraints. The most important ingredient of a successful private infrastructure investment is the careful *ex-ante* evaluation and assignment of the different types of risks. Risks should be assigned to those parties most capable of assuming them: governments should, in principle, stay away from commercial risk but bear in full the political and regulatory risk.

In drafting contractual provisions, care should be taken that the state/regulator does not become captive to the private partner's interests. Provisions should be made to ensure the continuity of the service in the event of the private operator's default or insolvency.

From the institutional perspective, transparency is very important in the process of bidding and drafting the contractual obligations. Regulatory functions related to the service provision should be clearly separated from the supplier. Transaction costs of tendering negotiating and finalizing an infrastructure concession might substantially decrease if the government assigns the task of these transactions to one specific, adequately staffed government department. Finally, it is important that special dispute resolution provisions be built into the contracts; reliance on the court system might only create additional costs and frustration in the event of future litigation.

In transition economies, private sector financing of infrastructure requires further efforts to develop the financial system. Educational efforts are needed to convince private parties of the opportunities generated from such projects. Another cause of the markets' shortcoming might be the underdevelopment of private institutions capable to bear longer term investment risk, such as pension funds and insurance companies. Supporting the development of the country's infrastructure is another important reason to encourage the development and active presence in the capital markets of such institutions.

THE PROCESS OF PRIVATISING UTILITIES

*Harry Bush**

Aims of privatisation

In the United Kingdom there have tended to be six key objectives for each privatisation:

i)   maximise value obtained for the taxpayer;

ii)   improve competition, leading to better quality services and lower prices for consumers;

iii)   improve the management of resources;

iv)   extend and deepen share ownership among United Kingdom public;

v)   create a perception of success in order to pave the way for future transactions; and

vi)   complete the privatisation by a particular date.

Often these objectives are complementary. In what are often very large flotations the steps taken to widen share ownership can assist in the objective of obtaining value for the taxpayer by increasing demand tension. However, some of these objectives can pull in different directions. For example, proceeds might be higher if a utility company were sold as a continuing monopoly; or there might be a conflict between the wish to restructure an industry in order to improve competition and the aim of maintaining momentum behind the programme as a whole. It is essential that thought is given in the early planning stages of a privatisation to the relative weight attached to individual objectives and the ways in which tensions between objectives can be diminished, so that the achievement of overall objectives can be maximised.

Introducing competition

In the case of the United Kingdom utility privatisations, competition has been of prime concern. Telecom's, gas, water and electricity were always perceived as "natural monopolies", so the introduction of competition in each case was bound to take time. The United Kingdom has taken a pragmatic view as to how this can best be achieved in the time that has been available for each privatisation. The approach has developed as experience has built up. Thus while the process of introducing competition has generally begun before the actual privatisation, it has also often been necessary to give the industry regulator powers to carry the process forward after privatisation.

---

* This paper was presented by Harry Bush, Head of Privatisation, HM Treasury, United Kingdom, at the eighth meeting of the Advisory Group on Privatisation "Privatisation of Utilities and Infrastructure: Methods and Constraints," held in Paris, 30 and 31 October 1995.

Telecoms

In the case of British Telecom (BT) in 1984, the company was floated as a single entity including the national network. The government of the United Kingdom took steps to allow competition to develop; in particular to maintain the opportunities for BT's fledgling rival, Mercury. The "duopoly policy", announced in 1983, which prevented any other company from operating a nationwide network with fixed links, was intended to provide an incentive for Mercury to develop its own network, as well as to give BT time to prepare for a more competitive environment. In addition, steps were taken to ensure there could be no cross subsidy between BT's network and other activities (*e.g.* BT was required to keep separate accounts for its network operation).

Many important steps leading to greater competition have been taken since privatisation. The duopoly policy ended, as envisaged, in 1991. The government White Paper "Competition and Choice: Telecommunications policy for the 1990s" set out a wide-ranging package of further liberalisation measures, including inviting applications for a variety of fixed-linked and other licenses. Since then over 80 licenses have been issued. Of these, over 20 are for public telecommunications operators competing directly with BT and Mercury. In addition there are 126 cable operators and four competing mobile network operators. In 1994 £4.4 billion was invested in telecoms in the United Kingdom.

Gas

As with BT, the privatisation of British Gas (BG) left the company intact, retaining ownership of the network. However, as a public gas supplier, BG was required to comply with any request for access to its network, and others were given the chance to compete on supply (except for small users where BG was given a monopoly franchise). Again, there has been further development of competition since privatisation. Reports by the Monopoly and Mergers Commission (1988 and 1993) and the office of Fair Trading (1991) led to the introduction of price regulation for access to BG's network, and put the operation of the network into a separate subsidiary from BG's trading operations.

Competition in the industrial and commercial markets has intensified and there are now 42 companies in competition with British Gas, who between them supply nearly half of all the gas used by industrial and commercial customers. It is also planned to end British Gas's franchise monopoly and extend competition to the domestic sector. This will be phased in on a regional basis starting with half a million households in the South West in April 1996. This will be extended to cover two million households in the South East and South West in 1997, with competition becoming national in 1998.

Water

There is no national network in the water industry and the 10 regional water and sewerage authorities were privatised as separate companies. competition in the supply of water has been limited to the margins of the regions, but the water regulator has sought to encourage "yardstick competition", comparing unit costs and water quality between companies. The privatisation legislation provides for restrictions on mergers in order to preserve the grope for yardstick competition.

Electricity

At privatisation the vertically integrated public utility was broken up to increase competition. In England and Wales the industry now consists of a number of competing generating companies; a transmission company who owns and operates the transmission system and is responsible for calling up generation plants to meet demand; and regional distribution companies.

The regional distribution companies have a monopoly of all sales to small consumers (*i.e.* those taking less than 100 kill) within their regions. Above 100 kW, the market is open and consumers may have contracts with an alternative supplier. Initially the monopoly applied to consumers taking less than 1 MW but this limit was reduced to 100 kill in April 1994 to increase competition. It will be completely abolished by 1 April 1998.

The position in Scotland is very different. The Scottish Companies remain vertically integrated and generate, transmit, distribute and supply electricity to final consumers. In Northern Ireland, Northern Ireland Electricity Plc is responsible for power procurement, transmission, distribution and supply. Generation is by other private sector companies.

As with the water industry, the regulator uses "yardstick competition", comparing unit costs and quality of service between companies in those parts of the industry that remain monopoly activities. He also has other powers to encourage further competition and recently obtained undertakings from the two largest generating companies that they would endeavour to sell 6 000 MW of coal and oil fired capacity, thus increasing competition in the generating sector.

Regulation of prices and quality of service

In the absence of full competition, some form of continued public regulation of privatised utilities is required to ensure that the interests of customers (in terms of price and quality of service) are protected. The framework established for the BT privatisation became the model for other utilities:

- the legal framework is set out by the privatisation legislation, including the duties and obligations of the regulator;
- the relevant government Minister is given the role of granting licences to companies operating in the sector, and óther limited powers. But for the most part the regulator is independent of government;
- the licence imposes certain conditions and duties on the licence holder (including on prices);
- the industry regulator has the duty of monitoring and enforcing licence conditions. He can also change the licence conditions if the licence holder agrees;
- if the licensee objects to a proposed change in the licence, the matter is referred to the Monopoly and Mergers Commission (MMC).

The specific price controls are matters for the regulators. The general United Kingdom approach has been to avoid the problems with rate of return regulation -- particularly the lack of incentives to reduce costs, and the fact that it applies to the whole business, not just to the areas where monopoly is greatest -- and instead adopt the price cap system, known as RPI-X, where RPI is the standard measure of United Kingdom consumer inflation. In practice, there is some overlap between the two approaches.

RPI-X caps are generally set for five-year periods ahead. These apply in the main to areas of utilities business where there is an element of monopoly (thus an electricity distribution company may have a separate cap for its distribution and supply business). This gives the licensee a degree of certainty, and an incentive to reduce costs since any cost reduction below that implied by the price cap is retained as profit. Consumers benefit both from the price control in the period concerned and, prospectively, from the incentives on the company to reduce costs because the savings feed through to the baseline for the next review. Without the incentive to improve profits by cutting costs between reviews, the scope for consumer benefit at the next review would be reduced.

Of course, RPI-X does nothing of itself to encourage quality. Indeed, the firm may have an incentive to reduce quality in order to save costs and increase profit. The government of the United Kingdom has therefore increasingly strengthened the role of the industry regulators in regulating quality. Under the Competition and Services (Utilities) Act 1992, the regulators were given powers to set overall standards of service and to require licensees to set up compensation schemes in cases of poor service. Such schemes are now in place for each of the telecoms, gas, electricity and rail, and information on service quality is now published.

Improving management

While it has often been necessary to strengthen management by bringing in outsiders with relevant private sector expertise, in many cases it has been the existing management that has carried the company through from the public to private sector and has been responsible for improved performance. Their performance improves for a number of reasons. First they are subject to clearer incentives, with increased emphasis on cost reduction, profit generation and customer satisfaction. Second, they are able to make investment decisions on more commercial grounds, no longer rationed by the need to compete for scarce funds with other public programmes, or diverted by political considerations. Third, they have more freedom to manage their businesses, distanced further from the political process.

Choosing a capital structure

The government's decisions on the capital structure of the business are crucial to the way that business is perceived by investors, and hence to proceeds.

There is a spectrum between:

- selling the industry with little or no debt (*i.e.* the government would write off any outstanding debt before the sale). This ensures that debt repayments do not impose any sort of burden on the industry's cash flow, leaving the industry with cash to invest, either-in existing plant or in new ventures; and
- selling the industry highly geared, with debt injected by the government. The standard United Kingdom privatisation legislation includes provisions allowing the government to adjust the debt profile.

The point is to establish the efficient level of gearing for a particular industry, which will depend on decisions as to how the industry is to develop in the future. In the case of the water industry, for example, where the industry needed to invest heavily to meet new EC water quality objectives, the companies were sold with low gearing to ensure they had sufficient cash available for capital spend.

Low gearing may also be the best approach where the government believes that the industry should be looking to diversify beyond its core business.

However, the impact of any particular capital structure on proceeds is uncertain; for example the effect of a low-geared structure may depend on investors, perceptions of the industry's diversification plans. If investors are satisfied that they will lead to profit growth, the value of the equity will be enhanced. On the other hand, if investors lack confidence, the price will be lower.

A surer way of obtaining value for the industry's cash flow is to leave it indebted to the government. Debt injected in this way matures on a regular basis, with the proceeds contributing to the overall privatisation proceeds. And the government can then sell the debt in advance of its maturity date, as it has done for BT and a number of electricity companies. So far, the government has realised in excess of £3 billion in this second way, and further debt sales are planned.

Sequencing of sales

There are three levels to the issue of sequencing. The first to arise is the question of the order in which to privatise different industries or businesses in different sectors. To a large extent this may be dictated by the readiness of the businesses concerned, in particular the competitiveness of the market and the degree of restructuring required. But consideration also needs to be given to the need to build up credibility and momentum. This may argue for one sale over another on grounds of public acceptance of the case for privatisation, scale relative to past sales, the scale and imminence of likely consumer benefits, likely interest of strategic investors and so on. All this implies careful appraisal of all privatisation options at an early stage in the programme, and argues for beginning preparations for later privatisations while the earlier ones are underway, so as not to risk losing momentum.

Within an industry, decisions on its future structure will be the main determinant of the sequencing of sales of the different parts. It may be necessary to ensure that various competing businesses are privatised in quick succession, in order to reassure investors that those remaining in the public sector will not enjoy any special advantage. In the case of the privatisation of the United Kingdom electricity industry, it was important to ensure that the sale of the generating companies did not lag too far behind the sale of the distribution companies, given the dependence of the latter on the former.

Where the method of sale is a flotation, consideration also needs to be given to timing in order to avoid other big offers. A clash of major offers, not just other government offers, is liable to depress demand. National Power and PowerGen were part-floated in a joint offer, because the risk of floating one ahead of the other would have had a detrimental impact on demand for the second. Similarly, in the secondary sale this year, the linked sale of part of each company ensured relatively even subscription for both, despite the freedom for institutions to choose one stock only if they wished.

Throughout most of the United Kingdom programme, a main concern in terms of timing large privatisation issues was the potential for clashes with other United Kingdom market activities. The position is now much more difficult with many countries seeking to privatise very similar ranges of business. Decisions on timing now need to take account of other countries' privatisation timetables.

Choosing the method of sale

The method of sale should, to a large extent, have been determined as part of the pre-privatisation stage, as it is bound up with the decisions on the structure of the industry and how it is to be regulated. The options are: a public flotation, an institutional offer, a trade sale, a management/employee buy-out, or some combination of these, including the sale of a strategic stake in advance of a wider sale.

The choice of method depends on a range of issues:

i)   the size of the businesses to be sold;
ii)   the public perception of the industry, and therefore the likely public demand for shares;
iii)   the overall objectives of privatisation (see above).

Although the UK privatisation programme has involved examples of each type of sale, the public flotation has been the dominant method used (in terms of value rather than number). This is partly because of the importance attached to wider and deeper share ownership as an objective throughout the programme, but also reflects the fact that the UK nationalised industries were mainly utilities, for which flotation is generally the most suitable approach.

Flotation

Privatisation has been the main element of the government's drive to widen share ownership (and thereby to develop the capital markets in the United Kingdom). The long-term decline in popular direct share ownership has been reversed and there are now three times as many shareholders in the United Kingdom as 16 years ago (over nine million up from three million). In the course of the privatisation programmer the government's advisers have pioneered flotation structures that have since become commonplace. Flotations of BT in 1984 (two million individual applicants) and British Gas in 1986 (4.5 million applicants) established new expectations for the retail market in the United Kingdom. In both these cases, but BT especially, the scale of the transaction in relation to what had gone before made it important to tap sources of demand other than the financial institutions. In the more recent sales of the government's residual shareholdings in BT and the power generating companies (GENCOs) the strength of retail demand had been established. Some two thirds of the available BT shares were allocated to private individuals; for GENCOs II it was over half.

The objective of widening share ownership has required the development of ways of maximising retail demand. A range of such devices have been pioneered. For instance:

i)   incentives for retail investors, particularly payment by instalments and bonuses for holding shares over certain period;
ii)   additional incentives for employees to invest in their companies;
iii)   high profile media campaigns;
iv)   clawbacks from the provisional allocation to overseas and institutional investors, whereby the proportion of shares going to individual investors could be increased if demand is very high.

As the track record of the retail privatisation issues has become more established, the government has reduced both the scale of incentives and of its mass advertising campaigns.

The process of bringing in retail demand has itself been privatised. Up to BT3 the government of the United Kingdom effectively depended on setting up a government-run share information office to market each offer, collect registrations, and process the applications. But for BT III and GENCOs II increasing reliance was placed on private sector financial institutions (referred to as "share shops") to perform these functions. By developing a greater role for financial institutions, investors became more familiar with the process of buying and selling shares through financial intermediaries, lasting customer relations developed and the share-owning experience was further demystified.

Maximising value for the taxpayer

Another important factor in the development of the structure of United Kingdom privatisation sales has been the various ways in which the government has sought to maximise proceeds by improving demand tension, reducing costs, improving pricing, maximising competition between institutional and overseas investors, and capturing the benefit from better than expected demand.

Instalments

A major feature has been the instalment structure. By asking subscribers to the public offers to pay in instalments, the price can be enhanced in two ways. First, the overall value attached by the market is less constrained by the available cash (and this applies at least as much to individual investors as it does to financial institutions). And second, the shares are made more attractive to some investors by the higher returns that can be made on the part-paid shares. Thus, although the instalment structure has been characterised by some as a loan from the government to investors, it has been used to increase the overall benefit to the taxpayer.

However, the government has also sought to realise the benefit of the instalment structure for the taxpayer by giving greater clarity to the economic value to investors. With the development of the more sophisticated "bookbuilding" approach to pricing an issue, the government has been able, in secondary issues, to assess the economic benefit against a market price and to seek to obtain this in the public offer. This was achieved for BT III and more than achieved for GENCOs II. But it involved a process of market education about the value of the instalment mechanism, as well as convincing investors that they should pay for it.

Fixed price offers and back-end tenders

The United Kingdom's initial privatisation flotations were constructed entirely on the basis of underwritten-fixed price offers. Such major fixed price public offers need to be open for a significant period in order to allow time for large numbers of investors to consider the offer and submit applications. The usual period is about three weeks. This introduces a pricing risk from market movements during this period, and tends to lead to cautious pricing at the outset of the offer to allow for downward movements. There are also underwriting costs to be borne.

In the later 1980s the government developed "back-end tender" mechanisms in order to be able to gain benefits for the taxpayer of excess demand for fixed price offers. In a number of sales (the first GENCOs and Scottish Electricity companies sales) provision was made for a proportion of the shares allocated to institutional investors to be withdrawn from the offer if demand exceeded a certain level and to be re-offered to those investors in a further open-price tender once the first offer was closed.

Bookbuilding

The United Kingdom's standard approach is now to rely on the process called "bookbuilding". Whilst this sort of open-priced approach leaves the government vulnerable to general market movements during the offer period, it offers the opportunity of achieving a price nearer to 'market' at the time. With bookbuilding, institutional investors are asked not just for indications of the price at which they might be prepared to invest, but to say in advance how many shares they would take at a range of prices.

Bookbuilding has also allowed more open competition between investors from different markets. In earlier offers shares were earmarked for different markets, but in more recent offers there has been no pre-emption by region. Investors of similar quality are treated the same regardless of provenance. This means that the government does not need to take a view in advance on where demand will be strongest.   Instead, a global co-ordinator appointed to co-ordinate separate regional bookbuilding syndicates, or to manage a single global syndicate, can ensure that members of the syndicates compete with each other to secure higher allocations from the total pool of shares allocated to the tender.

The bookbuilding approach used for the sale of residual holdings in BT and the GENCOs involved an open-priced public offer run in parallel to, rather than after, the tender. Both institutions and members of the public were invited to subscribe taking whatever price would be established by the bookbuilding. Subscribers were, however, given certainty as to the initial cost of the shares, in that the amount of the first two of three instalments was fixed in advance of the offer. Only the amount of the final instalment would vary depending on the price established. That had the presentational advantage of creating a degree of certainty for prospective investors about the cost of subscription to the offer, while leaving the overall amount uncertain. This allowed the price for both parts of the offer to be fixed on the basis of the current value as established by the bookbuilding.

Clawbacks

Although primarily aimed at maximising the proportion of shares going to individual investors, the clawback arrangements also increase demand pressure by increasing the perceived scarcity of shares available for institutional investors. This feeds into the pricing through the bookbuilding.

Thus there has been a gradual, but steady evolution of the United Kingdom pricing mechanisms through the large sales. Developments have been particularly marked in the sales of the residual shareholdings in BT and the GENCOs.

Trade sales

While the highest profile privatisations have been flotations, a great many businesses have been privatised by means of trade sales (*e.g.* Rover, Royal Ordinance, British Rail maintenance depots). The main consideration between flotation and trade sale is size. If a business is big enough to float, the objective of wider share ownership argues in favour of flotation. Moreover, it may not be feasible to realise the full value of a big business through a sale to a single investor. Trade sales are not generally appropriate for privatisation of utilities, mainly because of the size of the individual businesses, but also because of the need to avoid concentrated ownership in the interests of maintaining competition. But this is not a hard and fast rule. It all depends on the proposed structure for the industry and the trade sales are being used in the privatisation of the railways at present (though not for the sale of the infrastructure company, which is to be a flotation).

However, a trade sale may be the better option for businesses which do not have an established good track record, and where the balance of advantage lies in a quick transfer to private ownership. Trade purchasers are knowledgeable investors, and are usually prepared to buy a business on the basis of their judgement of management reforms already carried out, rather than waiting for the benefits of such reforms feeding through to the accounts.

Where it has been decided that a major restructuring of an industry into small discrete units is required prior to privatisation in order to create the right competitive framework, a series of trade sales may represent the best way to achieve a sustainable industry structure.

The basic approach to a trade sale by government is the same as for many *intra*-public sector transactions: open competition, a period of due diligence by prospective purchasers and one-to-one negotiations. Equally, they are just like trade sales between private sector businesses. As a private contract sale, there are no statutory disclosure requirements in the United Kingdom, so the vendor can judge the level of disclosure that will best serve the objectives of the sale. It is, however, just as important that information given to prospective buyers be accurate as it is for a flotation. The government's aim from the trade sale is to maximise proceeds from the sale and minimise the liabilities which are retained in the public sector.

Management/employee buy-outs (MEBOs)

MEBOs are simply a particular class of trade sale, where the winning bidder is a company in which the management and employees have a substantial stake. In principle, a bid from the management and employees is no different from any other bid, and should be assessed against the objectives for the sale in the same way. it does raise some particular issues, however.

MEBO bids are welcome because they increase competition, help maximise proceeds and can be useful in maintaining the commitment of the management and staff to the business in the run-up to the sale. If they are successful, the privatised business can benefit from the continued commitment of its staff. But there is a downside. Where there is a MEBO, the vendor needs to take steps to ensure that the business is run in a proper, objective manner, and not in some way that favours the MEBO. In particular, there is a danger that the business will be run in such a way as to depress the price or discourage interest from outside bidders. And while a MEBO may enjoy the initial advantage of inside knowledge of the existing business, it may lack the commercial management expertise to prosper following privatisation.

Public scrutiny of MEBOs is also likely to be particularly close where members of the management team have played a prominent role in advising Ministers on the privatisation. So particular care is needed in such cases.

Retaining residual control

There are various reasons why it may be attractive to retain a stake in a privatised company; either to retain a say in its future running -- especially where the industry has particular strategic importance to the economy or national security -- or because a staged sale would improve the net benefit to taxpayers. Where the concern has been strategic, rather than fiscal, a number of different approaches have been developed in different countries:

i)   retention of a significant residual stake;

ii)   retention of a special or golden share;

iii)   ensuring a hard core of strategic (usually domestic) investors (*noyaux durs*).

A main objective of the United Kingdom government's privatisations has been the transfer of the business concerned to the private sector where it can be subject to commercial disciplines and to market pressures. The general policy has therefore been to dispose of 100 per cent of each business -- either in one go, or in tranches -- relying on special shares where there has been perceived to be a reason for doing so (see below). Two notable exceptions were BT and the GENCOs, where residual shareholdings were initially retained of 49 per cent and 40 per cent respectively. But in neither case was it intended that the government hold a long-term strategic stake.

With BT the decision to hold onto 49 per cent reflected the scale of the sale, which dwarfed anything that had gone before, and the initial sale of the GENCOs closely followed the very large sale of the regional electricity distribution companies. In both cases, effectively all of the remaining shares have since been sold, and the staged approach has allowed the government to obtain greater value for the businesses as a whole because of their improved performance since their initial privatisation.

Managing residual shares

In the case of both BTs and the GENCOs undertakings were given in the Prospectus that the government would not "use its rights as an ordinary shareholder to intervene in the commercial decisions" of the companies. These undertakings were given because the government wanted to subject the businesses to private sector disciplines, and so it made no sense to have government exercising such a substantial shareholding. Indeed, although the sale of 51 per cent of the stock was enough to be deemed to have given away control (for the purpose of national accounts classification), this might have been called into question if the government had sought to exercise influence. The undertakings were designed to reassure investors that the future direction and management of the business would be in the hands of the directors and the private shareholders, and so to improve proceeds.

The industries were privatised with boards which had been appointed by the government, but once privatised their responsibility was to the shareholders. In some cases, mainly the defence industries, the government also retained the right to appoint government directors. This was the case for BT until the government relinquished this right along with its residual stake.

Subsequent sales of residual shares

Undertakings were also given in the original prospectuses for BT and the GENCOs that the residual holdings would not be sold for a number of years. This was to provide reassurance to the initial investors that the government would not dump its stock on the market in an unplanned and opportunistic fashion. However, the prospectuses also made clear that thereafter it was government policy to sell the residual stakes "as the circumstances of the companies and other conditions permit".

The government's objectives in disposing of the residual shareholdings were the same as in the original sales, but a new feature was the existence of a market price. While to some extent this made pricing rather easier, it also meant there was scope for investors to trade against the government by selling shares in advance of the offer, with a view to buying them back in the offer at a cheaper price, or by "short selling" (*i.e.* selling shares they do not own with the intention of buying shares more cheaply in the offer in order to settle the transaction). The government did not wish to depress normal market activity, but wished to deter investors from engaging in this sort of activity at the expense of the Exchequer. Three steps were therefore taken:

i) the precise timing of the sale was kept uncertain for as long as possible, and the government reserved the right to sell all or only a proportion of the residual holding. The risk that cheaper shares might not be available to settle the short-selling was a strong disincentive;

ii) the government announced that with the assistance of the global co-ordinator and other bookbuilding syndicate members, it would monitor market activity and reserved the right to reduce or eliminate the allocation of anyone suspected of manipulation;

iii) investors who were supportive shareholders -- *i.e.* they were judged by the syndicate managers and the Treasury to have a good record for holding onto the shares they bought in such issues -- were offered the prospect of increased allocations. This was done on the basis of a points system operated by the global co-ordinators. The government also made clear that it would reduce or eliminate the allocation for any institutions which appeared to have been engaged in trading against the government ahead of the offer.

Special shares

The government of the United Kingdom has used Special Shares in a number of privatisations where there has been a need to protect a business from takeover, for example on national security grounds, or where there is a special need to maintain independence for competition reasons (*e.g.* the special share in the National Grid prevents any one investor from controlling more than 15 per cent of the grid), or as a temporary measure to allow the management time to adjust to the private sector.

Given the aim of maximising commercial discipline, the remaining government interest has been narrowly defined and exercisable only within a framework that ensures that both the strategic and day-to-day control of the business concerned rests with the private sector owners and managers. The use of Special Shares should be the exception, not the rule. There are currently 18 Special Shares in place, primarily in the electricity generating and transmission industries and certain defence and telecommunications companies, which is a small proportion of the 48 major businesses and dozens of smaller ones which have been privatised in the programme.

Where there is a security dimension, the Special Share is likely to be long-term or indefinite ("timeless"), unless security priorities change. Where there is no security dimension the Share has usually been a temporary arrangement ("time-limited") , though an exception is the National Grid where there is likely to be an on-going need to preserve its independence. It is important that Special Shares be time-limited wherever possible, and should in any case have their continued existence subject to review.

Where Special Shares are agreed to be necessary it is important that they should avoid provisions enabling the government to interfere in the general conduct of the privatised business. The exact powers should be determined by the circumstances of the company in question but should be limited to the minimum necessary to secure the relevant objectives. Typical special share provisions include:

i) a power for the holder to redeem the share at any time for its face value (usually £1);

ii) a limit on shareholdings by any one person, or group of persons acting in concert, to 15 per cent (29.5 per cent for the defence industries), with powers for the board of Directors to disenfranchise any shareholder in breach of this limit to the extent of the excess;

iii) in two cases (Rolls Royce and BAe) specific limits on foreign shareholdings because of the security implications of foreign ownership of defence industries;

iv) a right for the holder to appoint the chief executives or other directors (now confined to privatised industries with a defence or security dimension);

v) a power over the disposal of material assets (seven special shares, again mainly in connection with defence or security issues); and

vi) a restriction on amendment of the provisions of the share unless there is both a resolution passed by the ordinary shareholders at general meeting in the usual way and the holder of the Special Share has given written consent.

Noyaux durs

This approach, which involves a "hard core" of nationally-based strategic investors to maintain the national interest in a privatised business, has never been adopted by the government of the United Kingdom. Any attempt to pick strategic investors for a privatised company can only be made at the expense of open competition between investors. Individual investors may also be discouraged by the prospect of a hard core of bigger investors pursuing a different agenda to other investors.

How should the government organise itself for sales?

In the United Kingdom the government's tasks in privatisations of the major industries have typically involved the following stages:

i) policy development and announcement;

ii) preparation and passage of legislation;

iii) restructuring of the industry;

iv) overseeing the sale.

In all these stages, the government Department with policy responsibility for the relevant industry has taken the lead in liaising with the company, appointing and working with external advisers to develop the proposals and advising the responsible Ministers. A Department will typically set up a team of civil servants to carry through a privatisation through the four stages above. The team will be relatively small in the first stage, but will need to grow significantly for the final three.

There are a number of sources of continuity or collective experience. The first, and arguably most critical, is supplied by the external advisers. A large proportion of the preparatory work for privatisation is conducted, or advised upon, by advisors who will bring expertise from other privatisations in different sectors and/or different countries. A second important source of continuity can be provided in the lead department, even where it has little or no previous direct experience, through the transfer of staff from other departments which have been involved in other privatisations. This is an approach which has been adopted frequently in the United Kingdom.

A third element of continuity has been provided by the Treasury involvement in all sales. The relevant Treasury team has tended to be the one which monitored departmental expenditure in the area involved, but there has also been an overall monitoring role played by the part of HM Treasury responsible for overall privatisation proceeds and policy. That part of HM Treasury has also gained a particular concentration of knowledge as a result of the sales of residual shareholdings between 1991-1995. It has been the policy that where an industry is privatised but not all the shares are sold in the initial sale, the residual shareholding should be transferred to HM Treasury.

Overall this structure has worked well for the United Kingdom, but there have undoubtedly been benefits from the degree of continuity of people involved in the sales of residual holdings by HM Treasury. Sales themselves, unlike the preparation and restructuring of an industry, all tend to involve much the same issues and procedures and experience allows individuals to more critically evaluate the professional advice they receive on each sale. By contrast, the earlier stages of a sale have been markedly different and it has been important that the team have specific knowledge of the industry.

One alternative way to achieve continuity is to establish a single government body responsible for conducting all the sales from the beginning. The relevant department could still play an important role in the policy and restructuring phases (though even then the industry may play a bigger role), but the privatisation agency would oversee the process, and would take charge of all the sales, and would engage the government advisers.

Another approach adopted in other countries is to charge the industry itself with the leading role in executing sales. Such a structure, however, requires a judgement to be made about the relative importance of facilitating the sale and maximising proceeds for the government. Unless the company itself has been made accountable for the costs of the exercise, or given a direct interest in the net proceeds, there would be no incentive for it to minimise costs and, hence, maximise proceeds. It would also not be appropriate for the management to act as both seller and buyer, so MEBOs would have to be ruled out.

REGULATION OF PRIVATISED UTILITIES: LESSONS FROM THE CHILEAN EXPERIENCE

Eduardo Bitran and Pablo Serra[*]

1. Introduction

Over the last twenty-five years, most economists have become dissatisfied with the entrepreneurial role of the State. Although the State has restrained public enterprises (PEs) from exerting monopoly power, the inefficient operation of most of them has resulted in significant welfare losses. PEs have usually been used for political purposes and this has led them away from cost minimisation. The driving force behind privatisation[1] of PEs is the conviction that attaining managerial efficiency in PEs a difficult task due to political obstacles.

Privatisation, however, does not automatically ensure the internal efficiency of firms. Agency theory shows that, in the presence of random events affecting the firm's results and risk aversion on the part of managers, there is always some sacrifice of the profit-maximisation goal. A highly dispersed ownership aggravates the agency problem. Information is a public good, thus a stockholder with a small stake in the company has little incentive to invest in the information needed to exert control over managers. The existence of strong scale economies in data-gathering accentuates this problem.

Ensuring Internal efficiency, however, is not the most critical issue in privately-owned monopolies. Profit maximisation leads unregulated or poorly regulated monopolies to charge more and produce less than what is economically efficient. Thus, natural monopolies need to be properly regulated in order to avoid welfare losses. On the other hand, very rigid or excessive regulations may result in firms' lacking the incentives to raise efficiency. Moreover, regulating privately-owned natural monopolies is not an easy task, due to its adversarial nature. Consequently, whenever possible, the role of the government should be to create the conditions for competition and leave it to the market to discipline firms. Finally, in a rapidly changing technological environment, the scope of natural monopolies is becoming more restricted.

Generally speaking, the process of privatisation plus regulation in Chilean public utilities has functioned reasonably well. Private utilities have invested large sums in expanding their services. The electricity service reaches about 97 per cent of homes. Since 1987, when the government privatised the main local phone company, the number of lines has almost tripled, from 581 000 in 1987 to 1 657 000 in 1994 (while at the same time rates have increased by 130 per cent).[2] These

[*] This paper was presented by Eduardo Bitran and Peblo Serra of Corporación de Fomento and Universidad de Chile, respectively, at the eighth meeting of the Advisory Group on Privatisation "Privatisation of Utilities and Infrastructure: Methods and Constraints", held in Paris, 30 and 31 October 1995.

figures contrast with those achieved by the underinvested public sanitation sector. About one million people living in rural areas still have no running water, and less than ten per cent of total sewage is treated.

The positive results of private utilities are explained by five main factors. First, the relaxation of investment constraints on public enterprises; second, the managerial capacity of the private sector; third, the isolation of public services from political pressures; fourth, a comparatively stable and impartial regime of contract law for privatised public utilities; and fifth, a regulatory system that encourages efficiency. The first three are related to the release from factors hindering efficiency in PEs; the latter two to the prerequisites for achieving efficiency in private-sector public utilities.

State ownership of infrastructure generates significant inefficiencies in investment. It is common to observe huge cost overruns in investment projects, and investment bottlenecks due to a lack of financial flexibility in adapting to demand changes. Political interference biases investment towards the construction of new capacity instead of maintaining existing capacity. Moreover, PEs' rate structures usually reflect social pressures instead of opportunity costs. Frequently, political pressures on PEs also result in labour rigidities. Incentive schemes with penalties and rewards linked to performance, although essential in modem corporations, are practically non-existent in PEs. In addition, it is difficult for PEs to suspend services to customers that do not pay their bills or to penalise those that pilfer services. Losses in public water and sanitation companies still exceed 40 per cent of production, whereas the main electricity distribution company has been able to reduce losses from 23 per cent to nine per cent in less than a decade.

The regulatory framework has a tremendous impact on the efficiency of privatised public utilities. Following Levy and Spiller (1994) we distinguish between the basic design and detailed design of a regulatory system. "The basic design of a regulatory system involves the mechanisms that impose substantive or procedural constraints on regulatory discretion and that serve to solve conflicts affecting these constraints." With regulators setting prices, utilities are vulnerable to administrative expropriation. Regulatory rules and institutions (*i.e.* the basic design) might be used to provide assurances to private utilities that their investment will not be administratively expropriated. If the institutional environment fails to do this, private utilities invest less than optimally in order to reduce their exposure to administrative expropriation.

As pointed out by Levy and Spiller (1994), Chile has incorporated substantive restraints into the detailed design of its regulatory system. Chile has highly detailed benchmark regulations with explicit mechanisms for resolving disputes between the regulator and the utility, with the Judiciary as final arbiter. These restraints are credible because the country has a long tradition of judicial independence that has restrained government discretion in areas of property rights and contracts. The only limitation is that the Chilean Judicial system has little understanding of regulatory issues.

The regulatory scheme has two goals: *i)* to compel private utilities to minimise long-run costs through the adoption of the most efficient technologies; and *ii)* to ensure the transfer of these efficiency gains to clients. The legislation mainly defines price-setting schemes based on the principle of marginal-cost pricing in simulated efficient enterprises (benchmarking), encouraging utilities to use the most efficient technology. Regulations in Chile take into consideration the fact that current natural monopolies could disappear in the future. Even in price-regulated sectors, licenses are non-exclusive. Furthermore, they establish obligatory interconnection according to prespecified terms. In addition, the development of an institutional regulatory capacity preceded privatisation: each public sector has its own regulatory body. Generally speaking, these regulatory agencies are responsible for granting licenses, calculating rates and monitoring the quality of services.

Even though the Chilean regulatory framework for privatised utilities is comparatively advanced, it still leaves room for opportunistic behaviour on the part of both regulator and firms. Recent rate-setting episodes have made explicit the problem of information asymmetry. Regulators had serious difficulties in gathering precise cost data from utilities. Another problem that emerged is the imbalance in negotiating power. The regulatory agencies are in a position of technical and other disadvantage with respect to regulated firms. Furthermore, because of their sheer economic size, utility companies have acquired an influence in the political system and in society as a whole, with which it is hard for regulators to contend.[3]

Although the privatisation of Chilean utilities has led to substantial improvements in their internal efficiency, these efficiency gains have not translated into lower rates, even after two tariff reviews.[4] The limited information and technical capability of regulators and the enormous influence of the private utilities in the ratesetting process, have prevented the full transfer of efficiency increases to consumers via price reductions, even allowing for significant time lags. This situation has led to significant increases in the profits of regulated firms in the electricity distribution and telephone services. Only in those cases where competition has emerged have drastic price reductions occurred.[5]

Consequently, two lessons can be drawn from the regulation of privatised public utilities in Chile (Bitran and Serra, 1994). Firstly, achieving competition, or at least yardstick competition, whenever possible, should be the main goal. Secondly, the speed at which the privatisation process is carried out should take into account the degree of progress achieved by regulatory institutions. These recommendations lead to less regulation, a desirable outcome given its adversarial nature. When privatisation leads to a competitive industry, there is no need for regulations other than those preserving competition. Also, the existence of autonomous and proficient regulatory agencies diminishes the resolve of monopolies to abuse their market power.

One of the most frequent sources of monopoly power are government regulations themselves. The Chilean privatisation process has maintained monopolies that have no economic justification whatsoever. For instance, the maintenance of most water rights in the hands of a single privatised power generator has imposed significant entry barriers. The long distance telecommunications company had licenses guaranteeing it a monopoly position in international calls. PEs should be stripped of these privileges before privatisation takes place, because it is disruptive and costly to change either property rights or regulations afterwards.

Furthermore, restructuring enterprises prior to privatisation should take into account the regulatory problems that will ensue. Regulation should allow for new entrants and recognise the fact that current natural monopolies could, due to technological progress, lose their monopoly status. Privatisation of vertically integrated and highly concentrated companies in the electrical sectors have created barriers to entry into generation and have restricted competition. The creation of one major local phone company which concentrates about 90 per cent of lines has prevented the development of yardstick competition.

A successful regulation of public utilities requires strong, autonomous, and technically proficient institutions, something that is hard to find in developing countries. Thus, the speed at which the privatisation process is carried out should take into account the degree of progress achieved by regulatory legislation and institutions. In Chile, regulatory institutions are governmental bodies, a factor that limits their technical capabilities due to low public-sector wages, and increases the risk of regulatory capture especially considering the high concentration of ownership seen in regulated utilities.

The rest of this paper is organised as follows. In Section 2 we review issues of managerial efficiency in natural monopolies. The third section reviews the regulatory schemes most commonly resorted to. Section 4 relates to the promotion of competition in providing public utilities. Section 5 describes the Chilean experience in regulating private-sector utilities. The final section draws some lessons from the Chilean experience.

2. Managerial efficiency

2.1 The agency problem

In large corporations managers and owners are, more often than not, different people. While we can assume that the owners' goal is profit maximisation, the management's purpose could be somewhat different. Exerting control over managers by shareholders becomes a principal-agent problem.[6] Principals (owners) find monitoring the behaviour of agents (managers) costly. When a firm performs poorly it is difficult for the principal to know whether this results from random events or from poor management. The agency problem is more severe in monopolies than in competitive firms. In the latter, it is easier to judge managers' performance by comparing the results of different firms. A mechanism that partially solves this multiple agency problem is to link salaries to performance. The optimal incentive contract requires managers and workers to be the residual claimants on the firm's profits. Nevertheless, risk aversion on the part of managers and workers, and imperfect portfolio diversification, make this solution inefficient. The problem is made worse by the difficulties involved in appraising individual performance.

2.2 Public enterprises

Many authors argue that the agency problem is even more acute in PEs than in privately-owned enterprises, and consequently there is a higher probability of finding large deviations from profit-maximisation in the former than in the latter. The owners of the PEs -- citizens -- exert no control over managers. Citizens are represented by the government, which becomes the principal vis-à-vis management. The government's goals could diverge from profit maximisation. It is common to see, in widely differing countries, how PEs are used for political purposes that cause them to drift away from cost minimisation. This problem is compounded, at least in LDCs, because public controlling agencies exert a formal but insubstantial control on PEs, introducing rigidities, but leaving fertile ground for corruption, especially in contracting with suppliers.

Private firms expand their capacity by raising funds on capital markets, and this imposes some discipline in terms of monitoring firms' managerial efficiency. Instead, PEs frequently obtain their funding either from the State or from the capital market, but with an explicit or implicit State guarantee. Thus, in PEs, market discipline is lost in the investment decision-making process. Moreover, white elephants are occasionally built for political reasons. Political interference biases investment towards the construction of new capacity instead of maintaining existing capacity. It is quite common to observe significant deferred maintenance on public infrastructure.

PE rate structures usually reflect social pressures instead of opportunity costs. Frequently, public utility rates are tampered with in order to abate inflation. In addition, it is difficult for PEs to suspend services to customers who do not pay their bills or to penalise those that pilfer services. Also, infrastructure overuse due to pressure of specific interest groups leads to premature

28

deterioration of capacity. This is quite common with public roads that are destroyed by overloaded trucks.

Political pressure on PEs usually results in significant labour rigidities. Incentive schemes with penalties and rewards linked to performance, although essential in modem corporations, are practically non-existent in PEs. Political meddling makes it almost impossible to dismiss low-performance workers. It is very illustrative that in many labor contract negotiations the PE workers' unions state that their only valid counterpart is the Minister of Finance. In a rapidly changing world, where flexibility is essential for competitiveness, labour rigidities impose a severe burden on PEs. Another related problem is the hiring of unqualified political appointees.

In Chile, some PEs were less prone to political interferences. These PEs were run by their managers, who usually constituted a technocratic elite, but in this case serious agency problems still remained. Management, which was quite autonomous in its decisions, saw its mission as expanding services, without verifying the social return on new investments. Also, the lack of competition made these PEs quite complacent, particularly in matters related to employment. But perhaps the most relevant fact was that many of these firms concentrated the normative, regulatory and production roles in one entity. Such a concentration of roles made managerial accountability difficult. A division of labour in which firms pursue profit maximisation and regulators only worry about allocative efficiency could lead to better results.

2.3 Private corporations

Policy-makers, aware that it is an almost impossible task to attain managerial efficiency in PEs, are resorting to their privatisation. Although there is an increasing consensus that privatisation reduces the agency problem, this reduction depends crucially on the ownership structure. When ownership is dispersed among thousands of small shareholders, with no one of them having a significant share in the company, there are not enough incentives to invest in gathering the information needed to exert control over management. Thus, managers in corporations with widely spread ownership enjoy significant discretion to pursue their own objectives. Shareholders, instead of exerting control, exert their exit right by selling their stock. Stockholders with transitory positions in a company, seek short-term returns. Thus, fragmented equity results in managers emphasising short-term goals instead of investing with a long-term perspective (Porter, 1992).

It has been argued that the risk of takeover disciplines management. This requires the existence of potential shareholders that could take control. They need to buy a substantial share of stock to control the company and capture a significant proportion of the benefits resulting from better management. However, the possibility of a takeover that would improve management makes it less attractive for shareholders to sell their stock. The free-rider problem reduces the chances of successful takeovers. The development of institutional investors (funds) does not solve this problem. Stockholding through funds creates a double agency problem, since the fund managers imperfectly reflect the goals of fund owners. For instance, they emphasise short-term profitability in order to attract new participants.

In short, if the alternative to public ownership of enterprises is diffuse ownership, where shareholders do not exert an active control over managers because of information asymmetries and high monitoring costs, we may expect improvement in managerial efficiency compared to state ownership, but privatisation will not completely match the goals of managers and owners.

3. Regulation of natural monopolies

In infrastructure it is common to see natural monopolies due to economies of scale and scope. Profit maximisation leads unregulated privately-owned natural monopolies to charge more and produce less than in an economically efficient solution, and this results in welfare losses. The government's task is to develop a regulatory framework that will curb abuses of market power, ensure the quality of service and encourage efficient operation of monopolies.

3.1 Regulatory schemes

In this part we review the regulatory schemes most commonly resorted to, by discussing their advantages and limitations.[7] The literature broadly distinguishes three regulatory approaches (Ordover and Pittman, 1993). The first one is an anti-trust agency that penalises market-power abuses. The franchising of natural monopolies is the second. Finally, price-setting by a regulatory body is the third approach. In most cases these methods complement each other.

Antitrust statute

An antitrust agency acts as a watchdog, penalising any substantial deviation from acceptable behaviour. Such surveillance leads monopolies to exercise self-restraint in exerting their market power. This kind of solution, if not combined with other forms of regulation, poses three problems. First, antitrust agencies have difficulties in gathering enough independent data to determine what the real costs of a monopoly are (i.e. they face an information asymmetry problem), especially considering that they oversee the whole economy, and therefore lack specific information about each sector. Secondly, even if the antitrust agency succeeds in the information-gathering effort, it still has to decide what should be deemed to be a market power abuse. Even well informed people could argue endlessly about what the adequate rate of return is for a specific industry. Finally, even if the tariff adequately reflects the firm's costs, anti-trust agencies have no means of fostering long-term even efficiency in public services. For these reasons, usually antitrust commissions coexist with regulatory agencies responsible for the approval or the setting up of new public utility rates.

Temporary franchising of natural monopolies

An alternative to the privatisation of natural monopolies, pioneered by Chadwick (1959) and Demsetz (1968), is temporary franchising. The idea is, in Chadwick's words, to promote competition for the field instead of competition within the field, when it is impossible to develop the latter. The franchise is allocated through periodic auctions, and usually the franchise is awarded to the bidder offering to charge the lowest price for the service. Between auctions, prices are indexed according to inflation.

The main difficulty in implementing this scheme arises when substantial sunk cost investments are required.[8] Here, two possibilities arise. First, the fixed capital may be owned by the government. In this case the problem is to ensure that the franchisee will adequately maintain the public property. The second possibility is that all or a substantial part of the investment is made by the franchisee. Here the challenge is to provide appropriate incentives for the operator to make the required investments. Dnes's (1991) proposal is that the new operator should compensate the old one for the investments made. Investments should be valued through a technical process stipulating arbitration clauses in case of disagreements. However, the valuation process once again leaves room for discretion. Fear of losing the franchise and the uncertainty involved in the compensation for previous investments could discourage the franchisee from investing.

A variation on the Demsetz proposal are long term infrastructure concessions via Build-Operate-and-Transfer schemes. In this case, the term of the franchise is long enough for the investor to recoup the initial investment, avoiding the establishment of compensation for sunk investment at the end of the concession. Nevertheless, price adjustment or renegotiation clauses are required due to the uncertainties involved in these long-term contracts, leaving room for ex-post opportunistic behaviour. This approach has been applied in Chile to the provision of public infrastructure in the transport sector. Traffic flow uncertainty on toll roads increases risk premiums dramatically, and this has led the government to provide implicit or explicit minimum traffic guarantees, thereby partly removing market discipline on investment.

Tariff-setting

The third regulation scheme consists of an agency that either approves or sets the public service rate structure. Here, two distinct approaches can be detected. In the first one the emphasis is on rates reflecting the firm's costs. In the second, the emphasis is on firm efficiency.

Cost of service price-setting. In this category the traditional regulatory mechanism has been rate-setting based on rate-of-return targets.[9] This scheme has been widely used in the U.S. for many years, but is slowly being abandoned. Since 1925 it was also used to regulate Chilean electricity, but often it was tainted by political meddling (Alé and Mallat, 1990). Price adjustment operates in the following way. When a company wants to raise prices, it files an application with the regulator, having previously computed operating and capital costs. The regulator audits the information and sets the rates that will provide the target rate of return in the light of demand information. This scheme has a serious handicap as it does not provide incentives to either reduce or minimise costs and it could validate inefficiencies through rate increases. In addition, when the target rate of return exceeds the cost of capital, this type of regulation can result in an over-expansion of capital aimed at increasing the profit flow.

Incentive price-setting. This scheme attempts to correct the main problems of the rate-of-return approach, by separating rates from firms' actual costs. The most commonly used approaches are price-capping and efficient firm modelling (benchmarking). In the latter, prices are set in such a way that an efficient firm attains a pre-established rate of return. Prices are reviewed periodically. In between reviews, prices are adjusted according to an inflation index relevant to the sector. The problem with this scheme is in obtaining the costs of an efficient firm. If only one firm provides the service, its costs will have a strong influence on what the regulator would consider an efficient firm. However, if there are many local monopolies operating under similar conditions, the lowest cost firm could be considered to be the efficient one.

Price capping (PC) was developed and first applied in Great Britain. This approach, also known as RPI-X, consists in placing a cap on rate increases, where the cap moves according to price inflation minus a factor X representing an *ex-ante* estimate of future efficiency increases. Every four or five years, X is adjusted. Any increase in efficiency beyond X is appropriated by the firm. If X only reflects estimated future productivity gains, this scheme provides the correct incentives to the firm.

A major advantage of this approach compared to the efficient-firm model, is that it only changes the rate at which prices move over time and not the price itself. This situation lowers the level of conflict in the regulatory process. PC regulation, however, has a serious limitation: there is no explicit mechanism for adjusting X, which in turn causes two problems. First, if the price is set well above average cost, the PC could lead to large deadweight losses. Second, regulators are tempted to consider past returns on capital in their periodic adjustments of X. Therefore, in practice, the RPI-X could tend in the long-run to a rate-of-return scheme.[10]

PC is currently used in the United States to regulate the telephone industry, but seldom as a pure PC. Most of the plans are implemented in combination with some sort of sliding-scale rate-of-return regulation *i.e.* if the firm's return goes beyond a pre-established band, prices are adjusted (see Braeutigam and Panzar, 1993). This scheme partly solves the problems of PC without eliminating the profit maximisation incentives.

3.2 *Problems in regulating natural monopolies*

Although some consideration is given to each of the three forms of regulation, the focus of this paper will be on price-setting. Next, the main problems that arise in regulating natural monopolies are discussed.

Costs of regulation

The regulation of natural monopolies is quite complicated, constituting a long-term contract between the regulator and the monopoly in which the latter makes significant sunk- costs investments. The existence of high transaction costs, precluding a complete specification of conditions in the contract, raises the possibility of opportunistic behaviour on both sides, which could result in significant resource misallocations. Moreover, regulations could impose efficiency costs on regulated firms due to lack of flexibility.

The regulatory scheme should have two goals: *i)* the price charged by the monopoly should reflect the firm's marginal costs; and *ii)* it should compel the firm to minimise long-run costs through the adoption of productivity-enhancing technologies.[11] These two goals are sometimes at odds, because a very rigid regulation to ensure that the firm does not abuse its market power could result in a lack of incentives to increase long-run efficiency, and raise regulation compliance costs. Regulations should also attempt to bring about competition when technological advances make this a possibility in natural monopolies.

Access to information

The regulatory framework should include disclosure rules, ensuring regulators an easy and prompt access to all relevant cost data, and specify sanctions for profit-shifting. The asymmetry of information between the regulator and the firm regarding production costs cloud all regulatory processes. Thus, the regulatory scheme should stress the regulator's prompt access to the monopolies' cost data. However, the best way to break down the monopoly on information is by creating yardstick competition among similar local monopolies.

Regulatory capacity

The strengthening of regulatory institutions is crucial to success in the privatisation drive, due to the specialised nature of their function. Regulatory agencies are part of the public sector, so their wages are bounded by public-sector wage scales. Public sector wages lead to hiring professionals with little or no experience, thereby generating conditions for a high turnover. Those that turn out to be more productive quickly learn the nature of the business and with few exceptions migrate to the regulated firms where wages are several times higher. Thus, the negotiating power of the regulator is unbalanced with respect to the professional capacity of the regulated firm.

Regulatory capture

Capture of the regulator is one of the main reasons for regulatory failure. Regulatory capture may lead the regulator to set prices and quality of services that knowingly imply the exercise of monopoly power. Since regulators may see their work in the regulating entity as a transition to the regulated industry, the risk of regulators being captured by the industry is high.

The asymmetric influence of utilities vis-à-vis consumers, in the regulatory process, facilitates regulatory capture. Utilities have significant incentives to invest in rent-seeking activities, while for individual consumers it does not pay to invest in information and a voice to countervail the influence of the utility. Organising consumers to invest in information, or raising their influence, could reduce the regulatory capture problem somewhat. However, for the same reasons that individual consumers do not exert proper control over regulators nor do they control group leaders. Large-customer associations would seem to be more attractive, and in Chile an association of large consumers of electricity has recently been formed.

Regulatory capture occurs more often when the regulatory process lacks transparency and openness of information, and the regulators are closely linked to the political process. Having regulatory bodies that are strongly dependent on political authorities encourages rent-seeking activities by the regulated and increases the political and social pressure that private utilities exert on regulators. On the contrary, increasing regulatory agencies autonomy from the political authorities should *i)* allow paying competitive salaries that would attract and retain able professionals, and *ii)* reduce the pressures and influence that public utility firms exert on the political system.

3.3 Regulatory and antitrust institutions

The existence of able regulatory and antitrust institutions, with the ability to efficiently regulate and promote competition in private utilities, is fundamental to the overall efficiency of the economy and for satisfying the basic needs of the population. Developing countries have to make a significant effort to strengthen the technical capabilities and independence of such institutions.

One issue that has been raised is whether it is preferable to have different sectoral regulators or a single regulatory body for all public utilities (see for instance Blanlot 1992). The latter option is appealing for developing countries given the scarcity of highly qualified professionals and financial resources in the public sector. The existence of common ground in the regulation of different public utilities justifies the creation of a single regulatory commission. The commission should take the responsibility for setting regulated rates, developing guidelines for investments, granting concessions, monitoring quality and interconnectivity standards, proposing measures to enhance competition, and protecting consumers' rights.

The commissioners should be selected from well trained lawyers, engineers and economists through an open process which guarantees their technical capacity and independence, with tenure going beyond and only partially overlapping that of elected governments. Such a scheme reduces the risk of capture, saves resources and assures a more symmetric intersectoral regulatory approach, thereby avoiding misallocation of resources.

Other regulatory agencies facilitate the task of the public utility regulator. Such is the case with securities regulation. Having efficient securities regulators to enforce regulations protecting minority shareholders will help to prevent any attempt by the controlling shareholders of regulated monopolies to circumvent the regulatory process by transferring profits to affiliated firms.

The existence of well staffed and well financed regulators, does not solve all problems. We can still expect conflicts between utilities and regulators. The regulatory agency cannot be a party and an arbitrator at the same time, hence, the need for a highly technical arbitration that certainly is not provided by the judicial system. Antitrust institutions therefore have important responsibilities that complement those of regulators. Some of these responsibilities are to clarify issues regarding uncompetitive behaviour by firms, enforcing equitable access to networks with natural monopoly characteristics, establishing conditions for market structure to enhance competition, for example by limiting vertical or horizontal integration, mergers or acquisitions in utilities. As regards measures to modify market structure, the opinion of the regulatory commission should be an essential factor to be considered by the antitrust institutions.

For other regulatory and antitrust measures there is the option of using the general judiciary system as appeal courts or designing specialist economic courts. The general judiciary system lacks the specific knowledge to solve the dispute properly, thereby increasing the uncertainty of the outcome. However, in ratesetting, ad-hoc arbitration processes can be established which would reduce uncertainty. The rules under which arbitrators operate are essential for the end result of the rate-setting process. Truth-telling mechanisms could be designed to induce utilities to provide more accurate cost data.

4.   Promoting competition

The above analysis shows that regulation is not trouble-free. The adversarial nature of regulation and the difficulty in obtaining precise factual information leads to a continuous negotiating game. The main policy implication of this fact is that the privatisation process should be implemented with great consideration being given to the intended aim of promoting competition whenever possible, and of avoiding situations in which natural monopolies could extend their market power beyond their own market by creating entry barriers in industries either upstream or downstream.

Issues regarding the vertical and horizontal integration of firms should be addressed before public utility firms are privatised, bearing in mind not only managerial efficiency goals, but also the objective of preventing the consolidation of private monopolies in markets that could operate competitively. By rushing into a privatisation process or neglecting due consideration to the relevance of fostering competition, the result in many cases is the maintenance or establishment of monopolies that have no economic justification, or otherwise the perpetuation of information monopolies which prevent efficient regulation. Concentration, the degree of vertical and horizontal integration and the number of local monopolies into which the industry is partitioned determine the barriers to entry, the long-run prospects of achieving competition in the competitive segments and the chances of efficiently regulating natural monopolies.

4.1 Removing barriers to competition

One of the most frequent sources of monopoly power are government regulations themselves. The maintenance of exclusive rights to natural resources, a lack of equal access to monopolistic networks, or simply granting legal monopolies in specific markets become leading deterrents to competition. Such barriers to competition are usually inherited from the PEs when these are privatised. The restrictions are kept because of the need to raise financial resources or due to a lack of understanding of long-term efficiency goals. Deregulation and the lifting of legal barriers to entry are critical for the promotion of efficiency.

Technological advances are continually reducing the number of activities which can be considered natural monopolies. Regulation should leave room for competition whenever technological breakthroughs render this feasible. For instance, the development of cable TV provides an opportunity to create competition in the local phone industry. In fact, cable TV networks could be used in the near future to provide local phone services. Recent mergers between telecommunications companies and cable TV firms in Chile illustrate this potential. The legislation should be flexible enough to accommodate an upsurge of competition in previously regulated industries.

Creating competition in regulated industries is easier when cross-subsidies between different services are avoided. A more efficient approach is for the government to grant targeted subsidies directly to the poor. Also, rate of return regulation precludes competition (see Levy and Spiller 1994). In fact, in a competitive environment it is not possible to assure a minimum profitability to firms. Braeutigam and Panzar (1993) state that PC regulation is probably most effective as a transitory step on the road toward total deregulation and fullcompetition. As services become sufficiently competitive, PC's are removed.

4.2 Equal access and interconnection

Equal access and interconnection requirements are essential for promoting competition in network utilities. Although the network itself could display natural monopoly characteristics, the supply of the service could, in certain cases, be provided competitively if access fees to the network and interconnection requirements are clearly established. For example, significant competition in supplying electricity to industrial users could be achieved if generating firms were allowed to supply them directly. The price of electricity for small consumers could be established with reference to an average of the freely negotiated prices to industry. In this case, the regulator only needs to set the proper interconnection and access charges. The risk of capturing the regulator is dramatically reduced, since generating firms and large consumers will both be interested in reducing interconnection and access charges. Therefore this scheme breaks the asymmetric relationship existing between the electricity distribution companies and the consumers vis-à-vis the regulator.

4.3 Vertical integration

When monopolies extract all monopoly rents in their own markets, they have no incentive to integrate vertically. However, if regulation precludes abuses of market power, monopolies will attempt to exert their market power in unregulated industries through affiliated companies upstream or downstream. Monopolies can discriminate in very subtle ways in favour of affiliated firms. This significantly raises entry barriers in the unregulated markets, leaving the door open to market power abuses.

Joint ownership of a natural monopoly and of firms downstream or upstream also generates the opportunity for circumventing regulation through transfer prices. Natural monopolies should be restricted to the provision of the regulated products, otherwise the regulation process becomes extremely complex due to the difficulty of sorting out the information regarding the operating and capital costs of regulated and unregulated activities. However, if there are significant scope externalities, restricting integration is inefficient, and an integrated monopoly should be allowed.

4.4 Yardstick competition

When the same service is supplied by different local monopolies, the information monopoly is weakened. This situation makes the efficient firm price-setting approach all the more appealing. For each firm the model could be the most efficient firm among the remaining firms. If there is no collusion, firms have incentives to lower their costs because this does not affect their own rates. This approach is most useful when all firms face similar conditions. For this reason, it is worth making an effort to promote the participation of different entrepreneurial groups in the privatisation process so as to ensure that electricity distribution, local phone service and water and sewerage are distributed among as many local monopolies as scale economies allow. On completion of the privatisation process, the regulatory agencies should prevent horizontal concentration through acquisitions.

4.5 Concentration

High concentration prevents competition in those market segments which are not natural monopolies, especially where these are vertically integrated with natural monopolies. Furthermore, in some LDCs public utilities represent a significant share of the stock market. Consequently, groups controlling public utility firms acquire significant political and social leverage, thereby increasing the difficulty of efficiently regulating natural monopolies.

All these issues of vertical and horizontal integration and concentration have to be properly addressed when deciding the restructuring of PEs prior to sale. In public utilities it is impossible to have competition without strong competitors, because of their sheer size. Hence the need to attract different entrepreneurial groups each having an interest in a significant stake in one privatised public utility. This requires legislation promoting competition and antitrust institutions that penalise uncompetitive behaviour.

5. Regulatory issues in the Chilean privatisation process

The purpose of this section is to summarise the Chilean experience in regulating privatised public utilities. Attention will be focused on the electrical power industry, telecommunications and water and sewerage services.

5.1 *The regulatory framework for public utilities*

During the 1980s, prior to the privatisation of public utilities, a significant effort was made to develop a regulatory framework through the introduction of new legislation. The legislation mainly defined price-setting schemes based on the principle of marginal-cost pricing in simulated efficient enterprises. Hence, a characteristic of the pricing systems was the distinction between peak and off-peak rates. In addition, the development of institutional regulatory capacity preceded privatisation. Each public sector had it own regulatory body. Generally speaking, these regulatory agencies are responsible for granting licenses, computing rates and monitoring the quality of services.

The antitrust system was modified greatly in 1973, when new legislation was introduced. This established that any person carrying out an action tending to impede competition would be punished by jail or fined. As examples of acts against competition the law mentions the sharing out of production or market quotas and price-fixing schemes. The antitrust institutional framework consists of an Attorney General for Economic Affairs and two antitrust commissions. The Attorney General is appointed by the President. The Central Preventive Commission and the Resolutive Commissions are made up of five members (there also is a preventive commission in each region).

5.2 *The water and sewerage sector*

The sanitation services sector underwent significant changes at the end of the 1980s and beginning of the 1990s. Until the end of the 1990s the provision of drinking water, drainage and sewage treatment was the responsibility of a centralised public service dependent on the Ministry of Public Works - SENDOS. In this period tariffs only covered operating costs and a minor fraction of the cost of investment, and the latter had to be financed mainly through fiscal transfers.

In 1989 and 1990 separate laws were passed allowing the state to carry out entrepreneurial activities in the production and distribution of drinking water, and in the collection and disposal of sewage. Under the new legislation Joint-stock companies affiliated to CORFO were created out of SENDOS: one for each region, thereby initiating the processes of "entrepreneurialisation" and regionalisation in the sector.

In 1988 a regulatory framework was established for these firms. This consists of a concessions systems covering both public and private companies. Concessions are granted for an indefinite period and are transferable. Four stages are recognised in the sanitation service: production, distribution, collection and treatment, with concessions being able to be granted independently for each stage. The legislation *i)* establishes the obligation of providing the service within the area of the concession, *ii)* defines rules of continuity and quality in the service; *iii)* imposes the obligation of interconnectivity with other sanitation firms when the regulating body considers it necessary. As well as this, in 1989 the Superintendency of Water and Sanitation Services (SWSS) was created, the entity responsible for regulating the quality of service and fixing the tariffs of the local monopolies. The SWSS depends administratively on the Ministry of Public Works. The rate system set up in the new regulatory framework allows for self-financing, including capital costs, in those firms which are efficient. In this way cross-subsidies are eliminated between the different sanitation firms. The new system of calculating rates was used for the first time in 1990, although rates were raised gradually between that date and the first semester of 1994. Along with the progressive rise, a targeted subsidy system was established for families of least resources, and financed directly by the government, up to a maximum consumption of 20 cubic meters. This replaced the old subsidy which was inefficient (users were not confronted with the real cost of the water) and regressive (it benefited more the families of higher income and higher consumption

As a result of the rise in rates, which on average were 80 per cent in real terms between 1990 and 1994, the CORFO subsidiary companies achieved an average profitability on capital of 6.3 per cent in 1994. There is a great diversity of results: profitability by firm ranged from -4.5 per cent to 13.2 per cent that year. In addition, arrears diminished from 7.9 per cent in 1990 to 2.9 per cent in 1994, as a consequence of better commercial management, a subsidy policy which gave incentives to prompt payment and the faculties granted to firms to suspend services to clients who had unpaid bills.

System of tariff calculation

The tariffs for each stage of the service and for each firm are calculated every five years on the basis of studies separately carried out by the SWSS and the corresponding firm. The SWSS formulates the basis for carrying out such studies. In the case of discrepancies between the studies, these are resolved by a three-member commission, two of which are designated by the SWSS and the third by the firm.

The methodology of the calculation is established by law. The rate is determined as the incremental cost of development. The incremental cost of development is defined as that tariff which gives a zero present value to investments needed in order to satisfy demand increases over a 35-year horizon. The discount rate used is that which is relevant to the sector. Rates calculated in this way are corrected so that expected income equals total costs during the period between successive rate-settings (the self-financing condition). These are readjusted whenever the relevant price index corresponding to one of the tariff charges accumulates an increase of more than three per cent.

Privatisation of water and sewerage companies

In order to take advantage of private-sector managerial capabilities and to raise the much needed financial resources to overcome a long period of under-investment, the government recently decided to privatise the water and sewerage firms which are subsidiaries of CORFO.[12] With this purpose in mind, it evaluated different privatisation schemes. The analysis led the government to conclude that the scope for competition in this sector was limited. First, competition in the production of water is restricted by natural resource availability. Second, it is unfeasible to establish an interconnected system, such as in electricity, for the transportation of water. Although competition is a possibility in the production of water and the treatment of sewage, its benefits are not significant enough to outweigh the transaction costs that would result from the breakdown of existing vertically-integrated firms. It therefore seems reasonable to allow vertical integration in the water sector. Moreover the inter-connectivity conditions imposed on concessionaires would allow the appearance of independent water producers if the case arose.

The government disregarded the option of keeping ownership of water and sewerage firms and granting long-term concessions, as has been done in France for more than a century and recently in Argentina, Mexico and Malaysia. Instead it opted for the full privatisation of existing vertically-integrated firms, as Great Britain did in the late 1980s. The main reason behind this decision arises from end-point problems in water concessions. As the end of the concession approaches, incentives for sunk investment and proper maintenance are increasingly reduced. Unfortunately, it is difficult to monitor the quality of the concession's assets because most of them are underground. This poses a significant problem especially when substantial investment is required close to the end of the concession. This stands in stark contrast to highway concessions where it is much easier to monitor the adequate maintenance of assets.

It has been argued that having a central auctioneer for local concessions would deter opportunistic behaviour by a concessionaire near the end of its term. Firms that have shown a poor performance in maintaining assets could be precluded from participating in future auctions. However, establishing an able central auctioneer does not seem to be an easy task. Moreover, it could become the source of endless litigation. The same entrepreneurs could bid in future concessions by using a different legal front. Furthermore, it would not deter opportunistic behaviour by one-period concessionaires.

In addition, long-term concessions would require periodical tariff reviews, given the dynamics of the sector. Therefore, granting concessions has few advantages over full privatisation. Short-term concessions do not seem to be the solution either. In water and sewerage labour costs represent a significant proportion of total costs, and so transferring the labour force between different concessionaires would pose significant problems. What incentives would concessionaires have for serious negotiation with unions, near to the end of the concession, if labour costs could be passed on to prices or the value of the concession?

5.3 The electrical power industry[13]

The regulatory framework

A new regulatory framework for the electricity sector was established in the 1980s. The new legislation introduced in 1982 aims at maximising society's welfare by establishing conditions for the efficient development and operation of the energy system. The National Energy Commission (NEC) was set up in 1978 and the Superintendency of Electricity Services and Fuels in 1985. Seven ministers sit on the NEC, which is responsible for computing rates and developing the medium- and long-term guidelines for the sector. The Superintendency of Electricity and Fuels, which depends administratively on the Ministry of Economy, grants the licenses and monitors the quality of services.

The Economic Load Dispatch Centre (ELDC), established in the 1982 law, co-ordinates the activities of generating companies. Its objectives, according to the legislation, are to obtain the minimum total operating cost for the system and to ensure equitable market access for all generating companies. The ELDC is made up of the generating companies and the NEC, which sees that the ELDC operates within the provisions and regulations of the law.

The electricity legislation distinguishes three separate activities: power generation, transmission and distribution, and prohibits the vertical integration of these activities. Competition is assumed both in power generation and in supplying large customers (those requiring more than 2 MW of power), while distribution (for small customers) and transmission are considered natural monopolies.

Consequently, the price system is made up of regulated rates for small customers and freely negotiated rates for the rest. The law specifies that the regulated electricity rate must be within a ten per cent band in terms of the average price of freely negotiated contracts.[14] Such contracts represent about 40 per cent of total power consumption.

The regulated price has two components: a node price, at which distributors buy energy and power from generators, and a distribution charge. The distribution charge is calculated every four years. The procedure consists of determining the operating costs of an efficient firm and setting rates which provide a ten per cent real return over the replacement value of assets. These rates are then applied to existing companies in order to verify that the industry average return on assets does not exceed 14 per cent or fall below six per cent. If the actual industry average return falls outside this range, rates are adjusted to reach the nearest bound. The operating cost of an efficient firm and the replacement value of assets are obtained as the weighted average of estimates made by the industry and by the CNE. The weight of the regulatory agency estimate is two thirds.

The node price is determined by adding the marginal cost of energy, the marginal cost of peak power and the marginal cost of transmission. The marginal cost of peak- power, which only applies to power demands during peak hours, is determined by the installation cost of a 50 MW gas turbine, as usually these are the marginal units operating during peak hours. Given the existence of economies of scale in the development of transmission lines, the marginal cost rates do not completely cover the total costs of transmission. The difference is charged to generators according to the development cost of the segment of the transmission grid used by them. The law is not explicit enough about how these areas are determined, and the charges are negotiated between the owner of the grid and the generators, leaving room for discretion. Recent lawsuits between generators illustrate this point (for details see Blanlot, 1993).

In order to provide more stable energy rates for small consumers, the energy price is computed every six months as the average of the expected short-run marginal generating costs for a period which varies between four and eight semesters, given the optimal path of expansion determined by the NEC, based on the investment program proposed by generators. Marginal costs are computed by the ELDC, taking into consideration the forecast future demand, the price of oil and coal, and water levels at the reservoirs. In determining marginal costs, the ELDC considers the operational generating plants independently of existing supply contracts. Energy transfers between generating companies are priced at marginal cost, which is computed quarterly.

Concentration in electric supply

The expansion of electricity demand leads to higher short-run marginal costs and this is reflected in higher node prices, thereby increasing the profitability of developing new projects. Existing enterprises or potential entrants invest in generation whenever a project has a return on capital commensurate with the sector's riskiness. Although the regulatory framework assumes competition in electrical power generation and in supplying large customers, the dominant firm in the Central Interconnected System (CIS) and its affiliates provide more than 65 per cent of power generation, own the transmission grid (which it manages through a subsidiary), and its controlling company - ENERSIS- owns the largest distribution firm, which concentrates about 50 per cent of distribution in the CIS area.

This ownership structure, in which a holding company owns the largest distribution company and controls the largest generating company, which in turn owns the transmission grid, combined with certain ambiguities in the regulatory framework, increases the risk for new firms which might be considering investing in generation. What is even more important still, the dominant generating company owns the water property rights of the most important future projects. Hence, by postponing the development of these projects it could obtain significant rents on its existing capacity.

Moreover, given that the distribution companies pay the node price for the electrical power and energy they buy, they are indifferent as to who the supplier is. On the other hand, generators prefer to sell when actual marginal production costs are below the node prices. Thus, a distributor could favour an affiliated generator by making contracts in which energy and power are mostly supplied when marginal costs are below node prices.

The introduction of natural gas from Argentina could significantly reduce the barriers to entry in the generating sector. The gas transport service has natural monopoly characteristics. Nevertheless, *ex-ante* competition between two consortia willing to build a pipeline to transport gas from Argentina, and anti-price discrimination clauses incorporated into the regulatory framework, are reducing transport prices to a competitive level. In fact, in order to obtain financing, the consortia need to have contracts signed with large customers. This has led to open competition for customers. Moreover, the possibility of both consortia building a pipeline can not be discarded, although this would make electricity prices plummet.

If the gas pipeline is built in a common carrier scheme, most future power projects will be combined-cycle gas turbines. In this case, the concentration of water rights will become less relevant. Moreover, power plants will be built close to demand, thereby reducing the impact of the transmission monopoly.[15] Nevertheless vertical integration between generation and distribution remains an important barrier for greenfield projects.

Setting distribution rates

Setting the electricity distribution value-added also has significant problems. The most recent price setting process (second semester of 1992) provides valuable lessons regarding regulatory frameworks. The fact that the costs of the simulated efficient firm are computed as a weighted average of studies carried out by the CNE and the firms, gives rise to obvious incentives for each party to alter the estimates. Discrepancies in the estimation of distribution costs and of the replacement value of assets in some cases exceeded 50 per cent. A better solution would probably result from an arbitration process in which an arbitrator would have to decide between the two studies.

Estimation of the actual cost of distribution was particularly sensitive. Distribution companies have diversified their business activities. In certain cases, vertical integration in the provision of inputs and services has taken place through affiliated companies. All this makes it harder to estimate the actual cost of distribution, allowing regulated firms to charge to regulated business costs borne by the unregulated business, or even setting artificially high transfer prices with the affiliated suppliers in order to increase return on capital beyond the levels established by the law. The return on capital in distribution companies and their affiliated input suppliers, or holding companies, in many cases has ranged from 20 per cent to 40 per cent, which is not consistent with the uncertainty of the business.

5.4 The telecommunications sector

The legislation regulating the telecommunications sector was introduced in 1982 and modified in 1987. In 1993 it was modified again to allow for competition in long-distance phone services. Since 1977 the regulatory body for telecommunications has been the Under-secretary of Telecommunications, reporting directly to the Minister of Transportation and Telecommunications.

Local phone services have regulated prices. The rate-setting scheme is based on the long-term marginal costs of a simulated efficient firm. The tariffs are set so that the net present value of expansion projects equal zero, when discounted at a rate reflecting the sector's uncertainty. Rates are adjusted every five years, and cost studies are prepared by the phone companies. Any dispute about cost estimates between the regulator and the regulated firm gives rise to an arbitration process whose characteristics are defined by law.

CTC, which serves about 90 per cent of local phone customers, has frequently been taken to the antitrust commissions. Some of the cases involve charging excessive prices for related services such as directory assistance or verifying the condition of the line for those customers that do not rent their phone equipment from the company.[16] There have also been long court litigations with minor phone service companies about whether or not CTC satisfies the connecting conditions provided for by law.

After its privatisation, ENTEL, the former long-distance monopoly, retained several exclusive licenses, which generated legal barriers to entry in the industry. The sluggishness of the regulatory authority in lifting these barriers and in granting new licenses delayed the emergence of competition. This, together with inappropriate rate-setting schemes, kept prices significantly above marginal costs for several years. In practice, the long-distance monopoly attained rates of return on capital which on average exceeded 30 per cent.

Recently, a law was enacted eliminating the legal barriers to competition in long-distance services, and Chile launched a long distance multi-carrier system in October 1994. This allows customers to choose from among eight different carriers in each phone call, by dialling three digits. The high profitability of ENTEL had provoked great interest in entering the industry. Five firms were ready to operate at the outset of the multi-carrier system, and since then another three have joined the pack.

What are the benefits to the country of a competitive telecommunications industry? It is still too soon to have a precise measure of its social benefits. However, certain preliminary information indicates that the gains could be enormous. Prior to the start of the multi-carrier system the cost of a call to the U.S. was more than US$1.50 per minute. Since then it has fallen to less than US 40 cents. The price fall has led to a substantial increase in traffic. International calls per month have increased from about six million minutes before the multi-carrier to around 11 million minutes since its inception. In the medium-term the demand response could be even more significant. For instance, Chile is aiming at becoming a regional financial centre. Low communication costs improve the chances of succeeding in this aim.

The counterpart of the consumers' gain is a reduction in the industry's profit. In 1993 ENTEL had profits of about US$80 million. If the first quarter results are annualised, the profits of all carriers will add up to US$15 million during 1995. These meagre results are explained by three factors. First, the dissipation of monopoly rents. Second, high, but transitory, restructuring costs to cope with a competitive environment.[17] Third, the disadvantageous position from which local companies have to negotiate accountancy rates with highly concentrated or monopolistic foreign carriers.

The accountancy rates are the values at which international carriers settle their traffic imbalances. Thus, a carrier with more incoming than outgoing traffic tries to negotiate a very high accountancy rate. Most accountancy rates are a multiple of the actual cost, thereby unduly raising the cost of international telecommunications. With an appropriate system for computing international rates, international calls should not exceed US 40 cents per minute. For instance, in Chile domestic long-distance calls cost about US 8 cents per minute.

It is interesting to note that details in the legislation could have a tremendous impact on the degree of competition in the industry. Local phone companies in Chile are legally obliged to allow their customers to choose the carrier in each long distance call, even if they have a signed contract with an specific carrier. Three digits identify each carrier, so using the multi-carrier is no more difficult than calling through the contracted carrier.

Local phone companies cannot disconnect the multi-carrier system from clients who have a signed contract with a carrier, even if the client requests it. Some phone companies have complained that this rule infringes personal liberty. However, public welfare imposes certain restrictions on citizens (long distance competition in this case).

Many public enterprises have licenses or property rights that guarantee them a monopoly position. This illustrates the importance of stripping them of such privileges before privatisation takes place, because it is disruptive and costly to change property rights or regulations afterwards.

The current law allows local phone companies to enter the long-distance service through subsidiaries.[18] We argue that as long as the local telephone service remains a natural monopoly, it will have the possibility of discriminating in favour of an affiliated long-distance carrier. It is almost impossible to achieve regulation that effectively prevents discrimination due to *i)* the technical complexities involved, *ii)* the lack of sophisticated regulatory capacity; and *iii)* a cumbersome legal system for settling disputes. Even if the phone company does not discriminate against its long-distance competitors, merely knowing its competitors' plans in advance constitutes a great competitive advantage (long distance carriers have to request new connections from the local phone company well in advance).

So far, our apprehensions about allowing the local phone companies to participate in the long-distance service through subsidiaries have been shown to be unfounded, although it remains an open question in the long-run. The long-distance firms want to enter the local phone service, ENTEL has made attempts to enter this market, so far unsuccessfully. VTR S.A seems to be better placed.[19] This company owns 52 per cent of VTR Telecommunications, which provides long distance services. It also possesses 99.5 per cent of VTR Cellular, one of the two firms that have a concession to provide a cellular phone service outside Santiago and Valparaiso. It also owns 73 per cent of Telefónica del Sur, which provides local phone services in the southern part of the country. This company, in turn, owns CNT Carrier, a minor regional company, and they control cable companies with about 50 per cent of cable subscribers. Their objective seems to be to jointly offer cable and local phone services. In addition, CTC bought INTERCOM, another of the major cable companies. It seems that the future will see competition between companies offering a variety of products.

When privatising telecommunications, care should have been taken so as not to grant monopoly positions through legal restrictions and exclusive licenses. The decision to grant CTC, the largest local telephone company, a license to operate a cellular phone company in its area of concession is also debatable, if its borne in mind that for technical reasons only two companies can operate in the same geographical area and, in the long-distance market.

6. Final remarks

There has been a subtle but noticeable change of emphasis in the Chilean regulation-deregulation environment since the country returned to democracy in 1990. The new emphasis is on promoting competition, including *ex-ante* competition, *i.e.* auctions.[20] Examples supporting this claim are the new regulations on gas pipeline concessions and the 1993 telecommunications legislation which has already created competition in long distance calls and will probably lead to competition in local services. This change is explained by the belief that technological change is rapidly reducing the scope of natural monopolies and the difficulties in regulating them.

In fact, the Chilean experience shows that rate-setting schemes, and regulating in general, constitute incomplete contracts between regulators and firms, raising the possibility of ex-post opportunistic behaviour on both sides. For instance, the law allows electricity companies to require reimbursable financial advances from customers requesting new services. However, the law does not say anything about the way in which the money is reimbursed. Rulings 792 and 793 of the Preventive Antitrust Commission asked the regulatory agency to specify the ways in which the reimbursement has to be made. The overlapping of distribution concessions is another source of conflict.

The regulatory process is increasingly becoming a bargaining process where the relative power and influence of interest groups is having a great impact on the outcome of the regulatory process. This environment has led to the development of rent-seeking activities, as it becomes profitable to devote resources to develop influence with the aim of favourably affecting regulators' decisions. Also, significant amounts of resources are devoted to settling disputes arising in an ambiguous regulatory framework between regulators and firms and among firms themselves.

The difficulties involved in regulation should generate a special concern for generating competition in privatised public utilities, as competition reduces the need for government regulation, although, in some circumstances, an active policy is required in the first place to achieve competition. For instance, enforcing inter-connectivity among all service providers is essential to achieving competition in telecommunications. The regulation of concessions -- for instance, imposing open access -- is required to ensure *ex-ante* competition in industries where it is likely that only one provider can be accommodated, as is the case with the gas pipeline. Reducing concentration in the electricity industry is needed to achieve competition.

The antitrust institutions are the cornerstone of a competition policy. For these institutions to succeed in their role they have to be independent from political pressures. Anti-trust commissioners should be full-time and have a solid background in regulatory economics and law. Also, highly technical and autonomous regulatory institutions are required. The Chilean experience displays two undesirable traits of regulatory agencies that are probably shared by many other countries. First, the unbalanced technical skill between the regulated utility and the regulators. Second, the closeness of regulators to the political system.

Regulatory agencies, as part of the public sector, have their wages limited by public-sector salary scales. Public sector wages enable hiring professionals with little or no experience, thereby generating conditions for a high turnover. Those that turn out to be more productive quickly learn the nature of the business and with few exceptions migrate to the regulated firms where wages are several times higher. Thus, the negotiating power of the regulator is unbalanced with respect to the professional capacity of the regulated utility. Furthermore, since the regulators may see their work in the regulating entity as a transition to the regulated industry, the risk of regulators being captured by the industry is high.

In Chile, regulatory bodies and the antitrust institutions have a strong dependence on the Ministries. This encourages rent-seeking activities and increases the political and social pressure that public utility owners exert on regulators. Thus, it is necessary to move in the direction of further independence by setting up regulatory and antitrust institutions which are more autonomous from the political authorities.

References

ALÉ, J. and G. MALLAT (1990), "Evolución del rol del estado en materia empresarial," in J. Alé *et al.*, eds., *Estado Empresario y Privatización* en Chile, Universidad Andrés Bello, Santiago, Chile.

BERNSTEIN, Sebastián, "Competition, marginal cost tariffs and spot pricing in the Chilean electric power sector", *Energy Policy*, August 1988, pp. 369-377.

BERNSTEIN, Sebastián and Renato AGURTO, "Use of outage cost for electricity pricing in Chile", *Energy Policy*, October 1992.

BITRAN, E. and R. SÁEZ (1993), *Privatisation and Regulation in Chile*, paper prepared for presentation at The Brookings Institution Conference on The Chilean Economy, April.

BITRAN, E. and P. SERRA (1993), "Regulatory Issues in the Privatisation of Public Utilities: The Chilean Experience", *Quarterly Review of Economics and Finance* 34 (1994) special issue.

BLANLOT, Vivian, (1993) "La regulación del sector eléctrico" in 0. Muñoz, ed., *Después de las Privatizaciones: hacia el Estado regulador*, Santiago, CIEPLAN.

BRAEUTIGAM, R. and J. PANZAR (1993), "Effects of the Change from Rate-of-Return to Price-Cap Regulation," *American Economic Review* 83 (2): 191-98.

CHADWICK, E. (1959). "Result of Different Principles of Legislation in Europe: of Competition for the Field as Compared with Competition within the Field of Service", *Journal of the Royal Statistical Society*, Series A22.

DEMSETZ, H. (1968). "Why Regulate Utilities?", *Journal of Law and Economics* 11.

DNES, A. W. (1991). "Franchising, Natural Monopoly and the Privatisation", in *Regulators and the Market: An Assessment of the Growth of Regulation in the UK*, in C. Veljanovkl (ed.) The Institute of Economic Affairs.

HACHETTE, D. and R. LÜDERS (1992). *La Privatización en Chile*, Centro Internacional para el Desarrollo (CINDE).

KLEIN, B., R. CRAWFORD and A. ALCHIAN (1978). "Vertical Integration, Appropriable Rents and the Competitive Contracting Process", *Journal of Law and Economics*, No. 21.

LAFFONT, J.J. (1994). "The New Economics of Regulation Ten Years After", *Econometrica* 62: 507-538.

LEVY, Brian and Pablo SPILLER (1994). *Proceedings of the World Bank Annual Conference on Development Economics 1993*, The World Bank.

MAYKEW, Ken and Paul SEABRIGHT (1992). "Incentives and the Management of Enterprises in Economic Transition: Capital Markets are not Enough", *Oxford Review of Economic Policy*, Vol. 8, No. 1.

ORDOVER, J. and R. PITTMAN (1993). *Competition Policy for Natural Monopolies in a Developing Market Economy,* mimeo, Seminar on Competition Policy, World Bank, April.

PAREDES, R. (1992). "Privatización y regulación: lecciones de la experiencia chilena" in O. Munoz, ed., *Después de las Privatazjones: hacia el Estado regulador*, Santiago, CIEPLAN.

PORTER, M. (1992). "America's Investment Famine", in *The Economist* 28 June. Extracted from *Capital Choices: Changing the Way America Invests in Industry.*

WILLIAMSON, O. (1976). "Franchise Bidding for Natural Monopoly: in General and with respect to CATV", *Bell Journal of Economics and Management Science* No. 7.

WILLIAMSON, O. (1979). "Transaction-Cost Economics: The Governance of Contractual Relations", *Journal of Law and Economics*, No. 22.

Notes

1. The Chilean privatisation experience is surveyed by Alé and Mallat (1990), Hachette and Lüders (1992), Bitran and Sáez (1993) and Bitran and Serra (1994).

2. This increase is partially explained by the elimination of cross-subsidies between long distance and local phone calls.

3. For instance, four out of the ten companies with highest profits are public utilities, and the holding company that controls two of the largest electricity companies is also among the ten companies with highest profits.

4. In any case clients have benefited from increased coverage and quality of services.

5. The Compaña de Telecommunications de Chile (CTC) tried to pressure the regulatory bodies during the last rate-setting by making catastrophic predictions about the effects the new tariffs would have on its profitability. The company's stock price abruptly fell and the Securities Commission had to suspend trading in them for a few days. Since then the predictions have not materialised. A similar situation occurred in 1992 with the main electrical distribution company, limiting the possibility of transferring to prices the reduction in energy losses which in part was due to the overall improvement in the economic outlook.

6. Corporations are complex entities with various layers of managers. The agency problem is repeated between top managers and second-tier managers and so on. At each tier the principal reflects in an imperfect way the shareholders' goal. See Maykew and Seabright (1992).

7. See Dnes (1991), Klein, Crawford and Alchian (1978) and Williamson (1975 and 1979). Laffont (1992) summarises recent theoretical advances in regulatory economics.

8. This scheme presents two additional problems. One is the possibility of collusion among bidders. The other is that the information advantage the incumbent franchisee has could inhibit potential bidders from participating.

9. There are other alternatives. For instance, the price could be set to equal the average cost plus a mark-up. Of course, if the mark-up is *ad valorem* this scheme has perverse incentives. This was the case in Chile for the legal monopoly favouring a sugar cane processing plant that went bankrupt when protection was lifted at the end of the seventies.

10. This possibility increases when a firm obtains substantially above normal profits. Abnormal profits could arise because of *i)* incomplete contracts regarding quality of service, product diversification, etc., leading to opportunistic ex-post behaviour, *ii)* unanticipated technical advances leading to productivity increases; and *iii)* under-estimation of attainable efficiency gains in recently privatised firms.

11. Natural monopolies have decreasing marginal costs, thus marginal-cost pricing will not cover the firm's costs. However, a connection cost, as in any two-part tariff structure, should cover the difference.

12. Investments tripled between 1990 and 1993, but they still are insufficient.

13. This section builds on Bernstein (1988), Bernstein and Agurto (1993), Bitran and Serra (1994) and Blanlot (1993).

14. This shows that the regulatory system relies heavily on the existence of competition in generation.

15. A generating firm -- Colbún-Machicura -- is considering building its own transmission line, and electricity distribution companies in the extreme parts of the SIC have forced ENDESA to sell the transmission lines in their distribution areas to joint ventures.

16. Ruling 754 of the Preventive Commission forbids CTC from charging, in addition to the cost of the phone call, for directory assistance on listed subscribers and asks the company to reimburse customers for previous charges (confirmed by Resolution No. 356 of the Resolutive Commission). Ruling 821 of the Preventive Commission forbids CTC from charging subscribers, who do not rent their telephone from the company, for checking the status of the equipment until the charge is approved by the corresponding regulatory agency.

17. The CEOs of four of the five largest carriers have been fired since the start of the multi-carrier.

18. The legislation imposed market share limits on both ENTEL and CTC Mundo during the first three years of the functioning of the multicarrier.

19. This company is controlled by the Luksic family, one the major economic conglomerates in the country which owns 50.7 per cent. Southwestern Bell recently bought 40 per cent of this company. The other 9.3 per cent is in the hands of Siemens A. G.

20. In the previous section it became clear that the lack of consideration of regulatory aspects before and after privatisation led to the monopolisation of activities that could have been developed under the discipline of competition. According to Parades (1993), this outcome is due to the hastiness of privatisation and the need to offer the private sector an attractive deal. Lack of experience in privatising public utilities in a country that pioneered the process in the region can also be adduced.

RESTRUCTURING THE NEW ZEALAND ELECTRICITY INDUSTRY

*John Wilson**

This paper sets out to describe the reforms to the New Zealand electricity industry over the last seven or eight years, and the reasoning behind those reforms. Although the restructuring has provided a number of new opportunities for private entry into the electricity industry, there has been no privatisation of the New Zealand government operations in the electricity industry. The government's policy is that there will be no such privatisation.

New Zealand economic reforms

The current set of economic reforms in New Zealand dates from the mid-1980's. The incoming government in 1984 faced a short-term foreign exchange crisis, built on top of long-term slow economic growth. Thus, while the foreign exchange crisis provided an urgency to economic reform, the longer term economic performance indicated that the reform should be fundamental.

The reform programme initiated by that government, and carried on and extended by its successor since 1990, has had a number of elements, based very broadly around the objectives of ensuring macro-economic stability, and promoting micro-economic liberalisation. The liberalisation programme has included a programme of removing barriers to external trade, reform of regulation to enable competition, and a comprehensive programme of public sector reform which has crystallised accountabilities in the core public sector, while transforming much of the public sector into either independent state-owned corporations, or into the private sector.

In the case of State trading enterprises in general, and of the electricity industry in particular, the seminal policy change was the passage of the State-Owned Enterprises Act in 1986. Underlying the passage of this legislation was the conclusion that, although by the standards of the New Zealand economy, the government had very substantial investments in commercial enterprises (some \$20 billion in 1985/86), they were in net terms producing no return on that investment. The reasons for that were seen to be:

– lack of clear commercial objectives and accountability;
– in many cases lack of a clear debt/equity structure, which would enable commercial performance to be compared with public sector companies;

* This paper was presented by John Wilson, Commercial and Financial Branch, The New Zealand Treasury, at the eighth meeting of the Advisory Group on Privatisation "Privatisation of Utilities and Infrastructure: Methods and Constraints," held in Paris, 30 and 31 October 1995.

– lack of the freedom to make commercial judgements, since new investments and wage and salary levels, as well as many other elements of spending, were subject to central government control;

– and finally, a confusion between commercial and non-commercial objectives.

The State-Owned Enterprises (SOE) Act set up these companies on a basis exactly parallel to privately owned companies, with operation of the company in the hands of a Board of Directors appointed by the two shareholding ministers, and with a clear objective of operating as a successful business. Scope for ministerial intervention in the company's operations is extremely limited. The State-Owned Enterprise model has formed the basis for much of what has happened in the New Zealand electricity industry.

The New Zealand electricity industry

There are a number of distinctive features of the New Zealand electricity industry.

New Zealand is a mountainous country, with regular rainfall, and with a population of a little over three million. The electricity generation system that has developed is thus dominated by hydro plants, although more recently hydro-electricity has been supplemented by gas-fired stations using natural gas from offshore the West Coast of the North Island, and by geothermal stations in the centre of the North Island.

The country consists of two relatively narrow islands. While the larger part of the population is in the northern part of the North Island, the best hydro development sites have been in the south of the South Island. Thus, the transmission grid, which includes an undersea cable between the two islands, is a crucial part of the electricity system.

Initial development of electricity generation and transmission was on a local basis, but by the mid-1980s almost all the generating stations and the national transmission grid were owned by the central government, and were operated by the Electricity Division of the Ministry of Energy. There was an economic licensing regime which would have inhibited the development of competing sources of generation. Distribution of electricity from the grid to end consumers was the responsibility of electricity supply authorities. In a few cases the supply authorities had developed small generating stations themselves. Some of the supply authorities were trading divisions of territorial local authorities, but the majority of them were elected local authorities in their own right. There was, thus, at that stage, no private sector presence in the electricity industry.

This paper will consider the history of the generation, national grid, and distribution industries since the mid 1980s, and in particular the growing scope for entry of private players into the industry.

Corporatisation of ECNZ

The Electricity Division of the Ministry of Energy (which, as noted above, comprised the generating stations and the national grid) was turned into a State Owned Enterprise (the Electricity Corporation of New Zealand -- ECNZ) with effect from 1 April 1987. The immediate effect was that the organisation was now structured as a company, with a clear objective of operating as a successful commercial enterprise, and that it had a Board, one of whose first tasks was to search for a chief executive.

While the purpose of this meeting is not to survey experience with corporatisations as such, it is perhaps worth briefly summarising New Zealand experience with the process to date.

In terms of purely financial outcomes, the results of corporatisation have been very positive. The return on the government's investment in ECNZ has risen to levels broadly compatible with private sector companies. At the same time, the number of employees in the company has fallen dramatically.

More specifically, some of the conclusions from a study commissioned by the Treasury to evaluate the ECNZ corporatisation were:

– The recruitment of key leaders is critical to the future of an organisation. In the ECNZ case the Chairman and the Chief Executive were crucial appointments. In that case they both came from outside the organisation, which helped the process of cultural change within ECNZ. The company's long-term future will depend on the continuing quality of appointments made to its Board.

– The change in governance structure involved in the SOE Act, and the freedom from detailed oversight from central government agencies, were both central elements in ECNZ's improved commercial performance.

– In the long run, while ECNZ is monitored by government agencies on behalf of Ministers, and while it is subject to oversight from the international finance markets for its borrowing, neither of those pressures are likely to replicate the strength of monitoring flowing from the tradable equity in a private company.

– The nature of ownership is likely to constrain any diversification of the business more tightly than it otherwise would have been.

The establishment of ECNZ as a successful SOE turned attention to the future of the industry as a whole.

Although ministers were of the view that ECNZ should remain in public ownership, they were increasingly of the view that some private sector presence in the electricity generation industry would be feasible and beneficial. The reasons for that conclusion were as follows:

– Although Ministers wished the existing generation system to remain in public ownership, they were by no means committed to the existing generator (ECNZ) building all new capacity, and to the capital investment implied by that commitment.

– It was concluded that competition in the electricity generation industry would help ensure that electricity was supplied at least cost to end consumers.

– More specifically, it was concluded that a variety of players would give a better prospect of allowing end customers to meet their needs through a variety of different contract forms.

By the late 1980's, attention thus turned to the impediments to new private entrants entering the electricity generation business.

The transmission grid

Clearly, any new entrant into the electricity generation business would require access to the national grid to distribute its production to end users. Post corporatisation, the national grid was part of ECNZ, the main electricity generator, and the dominant competitor for any new entrants. The task force which advised on the initial structure of ECNZ recommended that, in order to ensure that there was no suggestion of ECNZ abusing its powers, the national grid should be separated out transparently from the rest of ECNZ. At the outset ECNZ established the national grid as a separate cost centre, but within a year of ECNZ's establishment, the national grid had been more formally separated as a separate company, Trans Power, wholly owned by ECNZ. The ECNZ Board itself saw this separation as ensuring that the electricity transmission system was "open to any party's use for the transmission of electrical energy and had a transparent cost structure. This was seen to be an important factor in establishing competition in the electricity industry in New Zealand".

There was still a desire on the behalf of both government and potential new entrants into the industry to separate out Trans Power more completely than was possible as a wholly owned subsidiary of ECNZ, in order to guarantee open access to the grid for all potential generators.

There was a good deal of work on how to devise a structure for Trans Power that reflected the interests of both electricity generators and electricity distributors, in the context of the basically monopoly nature of the grid.

In 1989 the Electricity Task Force recommended that the grid should be owned by a "club", established under the Companies Act, of generators and distributors, with the government holding a "golden share" which could have given it special powers in respect of share ownership, board appointments, etc.

Regulation was to have been by way of information disclosure with recourse to the Commerce Act. An Establishment Board was appointed in July 1990 with the objective of establishing Trans Power on a "club" basis by 1 July 1991. The rationale for the "club" was that, in the context of New Zealand's light-handed approach to regulation, it would have allowed for the efficiency gains from private shareholder monitoring, while at the time ensuring that the interests of both producers and consumers were properly reflected in the outcomes.

A change of government intervened and the issues were reviewed, but in 1992 the new government again announced its intention of establishing Trans Power on a "club" basis by June 1993.

The discussions between the government and distributors did not produce agreement on the basis for establishing Trans Power as a "club". The reasons for that were:

- Some of the Electricity supply authorities were engaged in litigation about their corporatisation (that process is discussed later in this paper). While they were engaged in litigation it was not clear whether they had the power to invest in Trans Power.

- Some supply authorities were reluctant to invest substantially in Trans Power at that stage. Subsequently their investment has been concentrated on either acquisition in the distribution sector, or in developing their own generation sources.

- ECNZ and Trans Power were still negotiating with supply authorities about separate contracts for energy and transmission.

Subsequent to abandoning the "club" approach, the government decided in early 1994 to establish Trans Power as a separate State-Owned Enterprise, and that was done with effect from 1 July 1994. That has secured Trans Power's independence, and opened access to the grid for new entrants. Aside from the standard light-handed regulation, public policy concerns about Trans

Power's monopoly status are dealt with in the formal undertakings between Shareholding Ministers and the Trans Power Board.

1995 Electricity reforms

Although Trans Power had been separated as an SOE, there was still a desire to consider the other elements of a package that would facilitate new entrants into the generation industry. There was a good deal of work by the government and the industry, leading to a set of government decisions in mid 1995.

In coming to its decisions, the government concluded that it was looking for two broad outcomes:

- pricing of electricity in a manner that signals the full cost of producing each extra unit of electricity, so that investors and consumers can make decisions which seek to get the most value from each extra unit of electricity purchased; and
- strong pressure on electricity costs and prices, especially in the areas of new investment, over the next ten years and beyond so that electricity producers are forced to find innovative, least-cost solutions.

The government concluded that these outcomes were likely to be best achieved by a process of sustained and robust rivalry, and in particular by:

- vigorous competition among electricity producers, including new private sector generators;
- contestability from energy efficiency options as an alternative to buying more power;
- providing buyers with a diversity of prices and other conditions for purchasing electricity on contract; and
- competitive disciplines on prices for electricity in the spot market.

The principal barriers to sustained and robust rivalry were seen to be:

- the high level of dominance in the spot, contracts, and new investments markets by ECNZ, which presently generates approximately 96 per cent of all electricity produced in New Zealand;
- uncertainty as to the role that governments will play over the next ten years and beyond in relation to ECNZ's pricing and new investment decisions; and
- the absence of effective market mechanisms which buyers and sellers of electricity can use to forecast future prices.

A number of possible approaches to this problem were considered by ministers, officials, and the industry, within the context of a continuing undertaking that ECNZ should remain in public ownership. Options considered but rejected included:

- Leasing out a proportion of ECNZ's power stations to private operators, while retaining them in public ownership. This option was rejected because it was concluded that the complex contracting necessary to implement it would have made it an impractical option.

- Establishing a monopoly wholesaler to purchase electricity from all generators. This option was rejected because it was concluded that the monopoly wholesaler represented a step away from a market and consumer driven system.

The option finally announced on 8 June this year for consultation with affected parties, and for implementation by 1 February 1996 is as follows:

1. *A new State-Owned Enterprise is to be established as a commercially viable entity and as an effective competitor to ECNZ. The new SOE will have a mix of hydro, gas and geothermal power stations, with hydro and geothermal development sites, and an appropriate share of ECNZ's rights under the Maui gas contracts.*

This will:

- establish a significant and effective competitor to ECNZ, starting with about 28 per cent of the market in MW terms and 22 per cent in energy (Gwh) terms;
- ensure that the new SOE will hold key development sites for possible new generation, and accordingly be well placed to further reduce ECNZ's share of the market.

2. *ECNZ was to conclude its already announced sales process for the Taranaki gas power project, subject to resource consents and to the objective of maximising value.*

This measure will:

- reduce ECNZ's market share by approximately seven per cent in energy terms and five per cent in capacity terms;
- introduce another independent competitor to ECNZ, which will provide competitive bench marks in regard to performance.

3. *ECNZ is to sell a range of small hydro stations, which are remote from its core business, subject to appropriate consultation with Maori as to Treaty of Waitangi issues. It is expected the buyers will be either local power companies or Maori interests.*

The sale of these stations is to be completed progressively in the ordinary course of ECNZ's business:

- In aggregate, these sales will reduce ECNZ's share of the market by approximately four per cent.
- These sales should provide the opportunity for management of these stations by persons attuned to local conditions and for the achievement of greater operating efficiencies.

4. *ECNZ will be subject to a restriction on the amount of additional generating capacity it may provide.*

The cap will prevent ECNZ from providing additional generating capacity unless non-ECNZ producers have first provided at least an equal amount of additional capacity.

The cap is intended to assist in ensuring that:

- the output prices of at least 50 per cent of additional generating capacity reflect the true costs, thereby encouraging consumers to extract the greatest value to them from additional electricity consumption;
- ECNZ's market dominance is reduced over time;
- vigorous competitive pressure on costs and prices, and a diversity of views on the technology, size, location, and timing of new generating capacity, emerges; and

– the government's fiscal risk is reduced.

5. *Additional generating capacity provided by ECNZ will be "ring-fenced".*

Ring-fencing will:

– restrict ECNZ's ability to cross-subsidise any additional capacity and help ensure that the electricity produced from additional capacity is priced to reflect the full cost of producing it; and accordingly
– facilitate competitive entry into the electricity market by other generators and suppliers of demand-side management options.

6. *ECNZ will put in place a contract offer mechanism to ensure that customers have the opportunity to contract with ECNZ for 87 per cent of its capacity one year ahead, diminishing to 30 per cent, five years ahead.*

This will:

– provide market participants with a reasonable opportunity to insure against incentives ECNZ may have over time to unduly influence the spot market;
– give greater stability to the new market, by reducing the extent of participants' exposure to volatile spot prices; and
– provide greater certainty as to how the market will operate, and help address concerns in relation to spot pricing by ECNZ.

The intention is that, in combination, these reforms should provide a platform that facilitates new entry into the electricity industry.

I now turn to consider two specific aspects of those reforms:

– the process for ensuring that the two SOEs in fact compete with each other;
– the implementation of sale of the Taranaki combined cycle power stations, and the small hydro stations.

Competition between SOEs

Competition between private companies with the same shareholder is unusual, but certainly not unheard of.

As noted above, State-Owned Enterprises are set up in New Zealand on purely commercial lines. They are expected above all to make a proper return on funds invested, and in doing that to compete vigorously with other players in the market. The experience to date has been that the SOEs have followed that model.

Thus, the continuing ECNZ and the new SOE can be expected to compete vigorously in terms of their day-to-day operations. The most likely difficulty would arise if one or other of the companies were to appeal to the shareholding ministers for an intervention to stop a competitive practice of the other company. Another possible difficulty is if both companies were developing new competing generation projects at the same time, and the government as shareholder was subject to lobbying.

Scope for intervention by shareholding ministers in the day-to-day activities of SOEs is strictly curtailed by the State-Owned Enterprises legislation and the Companies Act.

Formally, boards of SOEs discuss their business plan on an annual basis with the shareholding ministers. The document setting out the agreed scope of business, objectives and financial targets (the Statement of Corporate Intent or SCI) is produced for formal tabling in Parliament. (It should be noted that if the company does not agree with the ministers about the Statement of Corporate Intent it may require that its preferred draft be tabled in Parliament, although that has not happened in practice). Beyond that, ministers powers are essentially that they expect to be consulted on major issues of legitimate concern to the shareholder, and have the power to object at that time should they wish. Their ultimate sanction remains the power of appointment to the Board.

Thus the two SOE models should produce vigorous competition on a day-to-day basis. It is possible that there will at some point be a conflict between the two objectives of maximising shareholder value and enabling broad economic efficiency. In general, where those conflicts have arisen in the recent past in New Zealand commercial assets policy (*e.g.* in packaging assets for sale), ministers have chosen to pursue the broader economic interest. Ultimately, the effectiveness of competition in the medium term will depend on :

- the extent to which the requirement for such competition is clearly expressed in the SCI;
- the quality of Board appointments to both companies;
- the extent to which ministers feel able to allow public competition between two companies over issues such as new developments. (One possible option is to have a different grouping of shareholding ministers for each of the two SOE's).

It should be noted that the companies will be subject to Commerce Act provisions about competition. In other words, the regulatory structure is exactly the same as it would have been for private companies.

Sale of gas development and small power stations

Although the 1995 electricity reforms have specifically ruled out privatisation of ECNZ and the new SOE, they did confirm the government's wish that ECNZ continue its plan to sell the development of the Taranaki combined cycle gas power station, and announced an intention to divest a group of small remote power stations. These two decisions were consistent with the approach ECNZ has taken of rationalising its peripheral assets. In that context, ECNZ had previously sold a small generating station and a maintenance company.

The Taranaki gas station and the remote power stations are relatively small parts of ECNZ's asset base. As such, just as with a normal company, sale of assets has been seen as the responsibility of the Board and management of the company, rather than the shareholder.

In the case of the Taranaki gas station development, the assets for sale have been some land with associated environmental resource consents, and a supply of gas. The supply of gas was not of itself sufficient to meet the project's requirements, and it was expected that purchasers would make their own arrangements for additional fuel supplies.

The sale process was that ECNZ set out an invitation to bidders, and the ECNZ Board made a selection from among those bidders. Ministerial involvement has been to endorse and encourage the process at the outset, and to be consulted at key points in the process. In the event the project has been sold to a consortium which includes a locally based company with gas interests, and an overseas-based utility which already has interests in the New Zealand electricity distribution sector.

For the remote hydro stations, it is also assumed that ECNZ, as the owner of these assets, would take primary responsibility for the commercial aspects of any sale. The government has announced, as part of the 1995 electricity reform package, that these stations will be sold to local power distribution companies or to Maori interests.

The first part of the process will therefore be a process of full consultation by the government with the Maori, to seek their views about whether the sale of the generating stations would have any impact on their rights as the indigenous people. That consultation must take place before government makes any final decision to sell the stations. It is required in terms of current legal understandings of the constitutional arrangements with Maori. The need for consultation is particularly strong in these cases because of issues about the basis on which some of the land was acquired for power generation.

If the consultation process allowed the sale of these stations to go ahead, it is likely that ECNZ would offer them for sale to local electricity distribution companies and Maori (with a partner if they wish). As with the sale of the Taranaki project, responsibility for the sale would rest with the ECNZ board, rather than with Ministers. As a general approach, the kind of sale that the shareholder would endorse most easily would involve a transparent process open to all eligible parties. In its own sales the government looks to have as clean a transaction as possible, without residual issues, and without any ongoing liability or ownership interest in the asset. While the detailed implementation of sale of these remote power stations would be over to the Board of ECNZ, the above sets out the standard against which the Board would be monitored.

Electricity distribution

As noted above, by the mid-1980s distribution of electricity from the national grid to end consumers, and retailing of electricity, were in the hands of electricity supply authorities (ESAs). Some of these were trading divisions of territorial local authorities, but most of them were local bodies elected in their own right. Aside from the state-owned electricity generator, these bodies were the only other owners of electricity generation stations. (They owned some four per cent of total generating capacity.)

Reform of the electricity distribution industry was informed by the same set of arguments as the reform of the generation system and the national grid. The specific aims of reform of the electricity distribution sector were:

- to introduce contestability into electricity retailing so that one distributor may be able to compete with another for the supply of electricity; and
- to improve the overall efficiency of the sector.

In that broad context, an Electricity Task Force reported in September 1989, recommending, *inter alia:*

- elimination of the legal protection for supply authorities' monopolies of both distribution lines and retailing of electrical energy, and the removal of the supply authorities' obligation to supply;
- tariffs to consumers of electricity should show transmission and distribution costs separately from energy costs;

- there should be no initial regulation of retail energy prices, and that regulation of distribution line charges should be light-handed;
- electricity supply authorities be restructured into company form;
- vertical integration between electricity distributors and generators should not be specifically prohibited; and
- supply authorities be privatised for listing on the share market.

These proposals were designed to enable private ownership of ESAs, thus giving them the benefits of private owner monitoring of their performance, and at the same time removing impediments to competition in those parts of the supply authorities' businesses which were in fact contestable (most obviously the energy trading function).

Several supply companies were corporatised at their owners initiative in the late 1980s. In each case the owners had come to the conclusion that corporatisation, by providing a clearer commercial focus and accountability, would provide a better vehicle for their shareholders commercial aspirations. In one case the supply authority also entered into an agreement with a US-based utility to purchase a 33.33 per cent shareholding in the business.

The initial response of the Electricity Supply Authority of New Zealand (ESANZ), the national body which represented the supply authorities, to the direction of change being canvassed by the task force was to oppose privatisation of ESAs and to oppose competition between them while there remained a monopoly generator. They argued that a removal of the regional monopoly accorded to ESAs would result in sharply increased electricity prices, particularly for rural customers.

Subsequently, ESANZ became more positive about the prospects for competition, and argued that ESAs should be corporatised with local ownership, most likely customer trusts.

The issue was delayed for some time by questions about the existing ownership of the ESAs and about the impacts on rural consumers. In a 1989 opinion, the Crown Law Office, the government's legal adviser, concluded that while the supply associations that were part of territorial local authorities (MEDs) were clearly owned by those local authorities, the associations that were controlled by directly elected boards (the Electric Power Boards) had no owner in the legal sense, but rather the assets were owned by the Board itself.

In 1990 the government decided that MEDs would remain in local authority ownership, and that Electric Power Boards would be owned by trusts, which would be directly elected by consumers. An Electricity Distribution Reform Unit was established to facilitate this process.

The Electric Power Boards Amendment Acts of 1989 and 1990 cancelled the Electric Power Board elections of 1990 on the grounds that reform of the sector was imminent, and then provided for the appointment of existing Board members as members of Trusts who would hold shares in the companies after corporatisation. At the same time, the legislation empowered the Minister for State-Owned Enterprises to appoint people with commercial experience as Board members of the about to be corporatised ESAs.

Following a change of government in 1990, a report commissioned by the Electricity Distribution Reform Unit in early 1991 concluded that private ownership showed the greatest potential for capturing productive efficiency gains, and thus recommended that the Electricity Power Trusts should transfer ownership of 70 per cent of their shares within three years. Ministers decided that each electricity power trust should be responsible for transferring ownership of the supply authorities to consumers, within constraints to be specified by the government. The government's decisions were enshrined in the Energy Companies Act 1992, and the Electricity Act 1992. Together, these Acts established the ESAs and local authority electricity operations as companies under the Companies Act, and required the Boards to prepare establishment plans, including share allocation plans, which were to be subject to public consultation.

The net result of this was that, at the time of corporatisation, some 50 per cent of the Electricity Supply Company shares were owned by community elected trusts, 25 per cent were held by local authorities and 25 per cent were in private hands. The proportion of privately held shares will have increased since then. Because the Trusts are required to review ownership periodically, and to operate in the interests of their beneficiaries in assessing proposals such as bids for their shares, there is a continuing move towards private ownership of the industry.

Several of the larger ESAs that proposed to distribute shares wanted to be able to list the shares on the New Zealand Stock Exchange. The listing requirements of the Exchange prohibited any provisions in company articles restricting the number of shares held by any one person. In order to get support for their establishment plans, however, these ESAs had all included provisions limiting the percentage of issued shares that any one legal person could hold. Finally, the issue was resolved by the exchange allowing for a special "Energy List". Companies listed in that way would be required to meet all listing requirements other than that applying to transferability of their shares. Companies would also be actively encouraged to seek elimination of restrictions on transferability, and the "Energy List" was to last for only two years.

Electricity reform: the results and the outlook

The objective of electricity reform in New Zealand has been to enable competition where that is practicable within the electricity industry, and to allow for private sector entry into the industry, without committing to wholesale privatisation of the existing state-owned electricity generator or the national grid.

Although there are no further major new decisions to be taken in the context of the present reform programme, the process remains as yet uncompleted, for the following reasons:

- The Electricity Supply Companies legislation was passed in 1992. That legislation has led to a great deal of ownership rationalisation within the industry, but that process, and the linked process of merger and acquisition, is still extremely active.

- Trans Power (the national grid) was separated from the generating company with effect from 1 July 1994.

- The government announced its decision about break up of ECNZ (the generating system) on 5 June 1995, but these decisions have been subject to consultation with Maori people about their rights. If, following consultation, the government decides to go ahead with the split, it will not be effective until early 1996. The sale of ECNZ's peripheral hydro stations, announced as part of the reform package, will not commence until 1996. While the sale of the Taranaki gas project has been announced, the new owners will not have that project completed for some years.

With that caution, the following broad conclusions can be drawn:

Energy Trading: This function, which comprises some three per cent of the retail cost of electricity, was at the start of the reform process in the hands of either the publicly owned electricity supply associations, or the state owned electricity generator. Consumers had no choice of supplier. Consequent upon the deregulation of the industry, consumers may choose from whom to buy their electricity. This choice is effective for mid-size and larger consumers. Energy trading is in the hands of the supply companies and of some dedicated and privately owned energy traders.

Distribution: The local lines business, which comprises some 27 per cent of the retail cost of electricity, remains effectively a monopoly. The supply associations were all turned into corporations with clear commercial objectives. Subsequent to that, a number of supply companies have taken on an element of private shareholding. Some companies have distributed shares to local electors, and in some cases the shares have been listed on the share market. Some companies have overtly sought outside cornerstone shareholding, while in other cases companies have acquired significant parcels of share holdings in these companies through open share market transactions. Several overseas utilities have been active in this restructuring. As a result, the number of electricity supply bodies has declined sharply. There were initially 44 ESAs. Some commentators predict there may be as few as ten once the present merger and acquisition process has worked through.

Transmission: The transmission system (which accounts for some 20 per cent of total retail electricity costs) remains effectively a monopoly, but it has been separated from any generator interests, and is thus open to all generators equally. The concept of the "club", which would have offered some of the gains of private ownership, while at the same time ensuring, because all interested parties were represented as owners, that regulatory concerns were addressed, remains dormant.

Generation: At present, ECNZ remains as a state-owned enterprise, the dominant generator. However, if the split of ECNZ goes ahead as proposed, and if the sale of the peripheral hydro stations proceeds also as planned, and on the assumption that the Taranaki gas station and other known private sector generation proposals proceed, then by the year 2000 the structure of the electricity generation industry will be as follows:

- ECNZ 64.5 per cent
- New SOE 19.1 per cent
- Private generators 16.4 per cent

That should provide the basis for the sort of robust rivalry between generators, leading to pressure on prices and a wider choice of contract structures, that has been the object of the reforms.

The Telecom sale

I now want to turn, by way of contrast, to how in New Zealand we have dealt with the telecommunications industry. The story here is one of regulatory reform and sale of assets. Both are representative of the general approach to government holdings of commercial assets in New Zealand over the last decade.

The distinguishing features of the Telecom sale were that it was, and remains to this date, the largest single sale of assets carried out by government in New Zealand, and that as a network industry there were issues of monopoly associated with the industry, and that it is one of only two cases in which the New Zealand authorities have to date used the "golden share" concept to achieve policy ends.

The government's involvement as an owner of the telecommunications industry in New Zealand dates from the 1860s, with the establishment of the Electric Telegraph Department. In 1881 that department was merged with the Post Office.

By the commencement of the current set of state sector reforms in the mid-1980s, the Post Office was a government department with three distinct business areas:

- telecommunications;
- the postal service itself; and
- a banking operation serving private individuals.

The Post Office was subject to initial State Owned Enterprise Act reforms in 1986 as described earlier. In the case of the Post Office, however, it was decided from the outset to establish three separate new state-owned enterprises along the business lines set out above. The objective was to ensure that each board had clear accountability for a particular set of business outcomes. The new SOEs were:

- New Zealand Post, which provides the core postal service, and continues to this date as a state-owned Enterprise.
- Postbank, which took over the banking operation, and which was subsequently sold in 1989 to the ANZ Bank group.
- Telecom, which is discussed further in this paper.

From its 1 April 1987 establishment date, Telecom as an SOE took over the assets of the Post Office's telecommunications division, and became the principal supplier of New Zealand's domestic and international telecommunications services.

The Post Office had operated as a legislative monopoly in this area, and at the outset Telecom had the same powers. The government began removing statutory barriers of entry to the telecoms market in 1987, and by 1989 the telecoms market was deregulated and open to competition. Telecom now has significant competitors in both the long-distance and cellular telephone markets. Telecom and Clear, its major long-distance market competitor, have recently reached agreement on an arrangement which will allow Clear to interconnect with Telecom's local network, and thus provide competition at the local level.

The government's attention then turned to the potential sale of Telecom. In 1989 a scoping study to investigate the potential for sale was commissioned by the ministers. Prior to that they satisfied themselves that, in broad terms, Telecom as an SOE was in a suitable structure for ownership outside the state sector, and that it was at least likely that the business would contribute more to national economic welfare under private ownership than under continuing public ownership.

The scoping study is usually a two-part process managed by Treasury officials. The Treasury appoints commercial advisers who produce a business evaluation. This report will forecast the expected valuations of the business under both continued government ownership and private ownership. It has assessed the commercial value-maximising strategy for the Crown as owner. If sale is part of that strategy, the report will include recommendations as to the value maximising sale strategy.

Using the business evaluation as a base, along with information gathered during its monitoring of the company, the Treasury writes a scoping report, which covers both commercial and wider public policy issues.

Following the scoping study process, and a commitment of Treasury resources to the project, the government announced its intention in March 1990 to sell Telecom. Total sale of the company was favoured. That was because the experience of the New Zealand government as a minority shareholder has not been positive. That is because it is difficult to properly monitor such share holdings, and thus the government is exposed to higher levels of risk. This is because the relations between the government and other shareholders rarely end up being symmetrical, in that the government usually accepts a higher proportion of the risk of the project than do the private shareholders, and because as a minority shareholder the government's position for any future potential downselling of its shareholding is weakened. Along with the sale of Air New Zealand, Telecom was one of the few occasions to date where a New Zealand privatisation has included a public float.

The government sold Telecom in June 1990 to a consortium of two of the US "baby Bells" (Bell Atlantic and Ameritech) and two local companies. The price was $NZ 4.25 billion, which at that time equalled $US2.5 billion. As an indicator of the significance of the transaction for the New Zealand government, receipts from the sale were equal to some 12 per cent of public debt at the time.

The sale agreement was structured such that the consortium purchased 100 per cent of the shares, but with an obligation to reduce their shareholding to 49.9 per cent within three years. This was to be achieved by the two local companies, increasing their initial small shareholding to 5 per cent of the company each over the next three years, and the remaining 40 per cent would be floated, including some $500 million in New Zealand. That transaction was in fact completed a year later than initially planned, because of market conditions at the time.

The broad approach to regulation of the newly privatised Telecom was to rely on the general competition/antitrust law. The Commerce Act, which is the main legislative vehicle in New Zealand in this area, provides for the threat of price controls, and has specific provisions at section 36 dealing with the potential misuse of a dominant position in a market. This is broadly parallel with the system of regulation for the electricity industry described earlier. In the case of Telecom, a general factor in the decision to opt for lighthanded regulation was the fact that rapid evolution of telecommunications technology meant that the markets in which Telecom operates would become increasingly competitive. The only exception, with high entry barriers, was the local loop.

Beyond that, the Telecommunications Act and its associated regulations provided for information transparency from telecom operators, in that they mandated a higher level of information disclosure than the companies would themselves necessarily have carried out. Finally, Telecom itself provided undertakings on price and service in the context of its "Golden Share" arrangements.

New Zealand is a small economy, and so the participation of foreign companies in sales processes for major assets is important, because it ensures a competitive and value-maximising process. Beyond that, overseas investors can bring in technical and management expertise, technology, and international linkages which further increase the contribution of the asset to the national economy.

Nonetheless, as in many countries, the New Zealand public is sometimes concerned about foreign investment, and in the case of Telecom this could have been heightened by a perception that telecommunications is a strategic national asset. At the time Telecom was sold in New Zealand, no other country had permitted foreign ownership of the dominant telecommunications company. These concerns were tempered in the early part of the sale process, by a recognition that a foreign purchaser of Telecom might welcome substantial domestic share holding as an assurance against future government policy changes.

As noted above, the consortium purchased Telecom in 1990, with an obligation to sell down their shareholding to 49.9 per cent by way of public offering. In accord with that obligation, in 1991 they floated 31 per cent of the company in the largest public offering in New Zealand. In 1993 the two American companies privately placed the remaining nine per cent of their obligation with institutional investors. The same year the two local companies took up their shareholding, and passed it on to institutional investors. A critical factor in structuring was to ensure that Telecom would be priced globally as a utility. There was a good deal of international interest in telecom shares at the time, and this would be the first such stock from the region. The amount of stock available in New Zealand was seen to be the maximum which could be absorbed without calling into question the objective of having international investors set the price.

Telecom golden share

The Telecom "golden share", known as the "kiwi share", works as follows:

The kiwi share is explicitly spelt out in the company's articles of association. The shareholder is the Minister of Communications. The share provides two powers:

Foreign ownership

The objective here was to establish a set of undertakings which enabled a foreign company to be accepted as the strategic shareholder. The provisions are:

No investor may increase their ownership to more than ten per cent of Telecom without the approval of the "kiwi shareholder";

At least half of the Telecom Board must be New Zealand citizens;

No investor may increase their ownership to more than 49.9 per cent of the company without the approval of the kiwi shareholder.

Price and service

This pledge was volunteered by the company to facilitate sale. The company recognised that private ownership was in its interests because it could enhance commercial performance. The company recognised that the public needed to be assured that an end to Government ownership would not undermine the quality of services. The pledge provided:

- The option of free local calling must be retained. (In New Zealand, local calls have not been charged on a per call basis. Rather, the cost of the local calls has been charged through a monthly charge. The "Kiwi share" provision thus requires Telecom at least to continue to offer a flat rate monthly charge for local calling as an option.)

- The standard residential monthly rental (as described above) must not increase in real terms unless the company's overall profitability is at stake.

- The charges for residential lines in rural areas must be no higher than the standard residential telephone rental, and ordinary telephone services must be as widely available as was the case at the time of sale.

In terms of enforcement of the "kiwi share" obligations, the Minister of Communications, as the kiwi shareholder, can enforce the sale of any shares which are held in excess of the limits set out above. The Minister can also enforce the price and service obligations set out in the "kiwi share" documentation through the courts. Finally, the government has the power to enforce through legislation.

The very clear intention, however, has been that the "kiwi share" should be self-policing. Because the overseas shareholders would be very conscious of public reaction to any breach of the "kiwi shareholder" provisions, and would wish to avoid any situation where the government had to respond to any public concern about a breach of the provisions, the expectation has been that any enforcement action over the "kiwi share" would only arise in an extreme situation.

The "kiwi share" was designed to be consistent with, and in no sense detract from, the company's ability to maximise shareholder value. As set out above, the approach to foreign ownership was based on recognition that foreign shareholders could bring more benefit than local shareholders, while the price and service provisions were seen by Telecom itself as value neutral. The government therefore saw the approach as being entirely consistent with its stated objective of maximising value through selling for the best possible price. Sale of Telecom without the "kiwi share" would have meant discounting the price very heavily to favour the New Zealand market.

While a restriction of ownership, or on the behaviour of those new owners, may entail a reduction in the price received for the company, the lessons as we see it from the "kiwi share" and the broader Telecom sale are that these effects can be mitigated if the restrictions are aligned as closely as practicable to the ownership structure that would be likely to emerge from a market driven sales process, and if the restrictions are explicit and focused to avoid any uncertainty.

INFRASTRUCTURE - PRIVATE FINANCE WITHOUT PRIVATISATION

Sir Adam Ridley[*]

Introduction

The essence of this presentation can be summarised simply. Let us look at the provision of goods or services in relation to (at least) three elements:

1. The *consumption* process, which may be mediated by *cash* and the normal market place or undertaken *directly* by producer to consumer, without a buyer or seller, prices or cash.

2. The process of *production or provision* of the good or service, which may be owned *publicly*; or *privately*.

3. The capital assets used in the production or provision of the goods or services which may also be owned *publicly* or *privately*.

noting also that:

4. Stages (2) and (3) can be monopolies, whether or not regulated or competitive.

The three pairs of possibilities (1) to (3) are illustrated in Table 1. There are, of course many possible combinations of them, in theory.

Table 2 illustrates the *classic process of privatisation*. A business *selling* goods or services in the *cash* economy is transferred from public control and ownership to private control and ownership. This has, of course, been one of the central preoccupations in OECD and CEECs alike since the Thatcher revolution and the end of command economies.

There are of course *other* kinds of activity which typically are still provided by public bodies directly to "consumers" rather than in or through the cash economy. In recent years much has been done to bring them into the private economy by means other than privatisation of the production process. This is illustrated in Table 3. Consumption remains *direct*, in most cases, *unmediated by cash*. Control remains firmly in public hands. But the *assets* are owned not publicly but privately, either wholly or partly, in some kind of partnership with the public authorities.

On the face of it, what is happening is little more than "contracting out" to private producers a function previously undertaken comprehensively in the public sector. However, this inference is wrong. Typically "contracting out" involves no more than the replacement of public suppliers of a

---

[*]   This paper was presented by Sir Adam Ridley, Executive Director, Hambros Bank Limited, London, at the eighth meeting of the Advisory Group on Privatisation "Privatisation of Utilities and Infrastructure: Methods and Constraints", held in Paris, 30 and 31 October 1995.

flow of goods and services with private sector suppliers of *those same flows*. Thus official documents once exclusively printed by the government printing works may be printed under contract by privately-owned printing companies. In contrast, the essence of what is illustrated in Table 3 is the replacement of a *capital asset owned* by the public sector by a *flow of goods and services* provided by assets owned by the private sector.

This is a trivial process in almost every sense when the assets involved are small and widely available in the competitive market. Closing down a hospital laundry and sending the work to a private laundry would fall in this category. However, even after the privatisation of the principal utilities, the public sector will still be a major investor; perhaps spending several per cent of GDP in OECD countries on roads, hospitals, schools, colleges, computer systems, prisons, defence facilities and so on. Much, or all, of this is *classic infrastructure*, procured and administered in what, even in the West, is a cash-free *command economy* particularly, but *not* only, at the consumption end. Private finance for such major infrastructure is not a trivial process.

Such talk of a command economy might provoke one to stop and think. One might ask why the liberal modernisers in the West have devoted so much effort to privatising entities which were already in the cash economy (*c.f.* Table 2) if not totally so; and so little effort have been given to the much more sheltered activities provided by what I have termed "classic infrastructure" in the preceding paragraph. Enthusiasts for competitive markets might also have been expected to target these activities early on. The explanations of this paradox are not obvious. one reason may be that the activities involved are *so* far from the market place that we have very few conventional economic or commercial statistics with which to appraise them. Perhaps more important is the simple fact that there was a consensus in informed circles that the well-established arrangements in these sectors were as good as one could hope for.

Be that as it may, the critics of "classic infrastructure" have been vocal for decades and the problems involved with its provision have become much more serious, often critically so in recent years. The following stylised synthesis exaggerates and stylises the criticisms but probably embodies most of the standard concerns. We shall start at the consumption end, working back through production to the underlying assets.

Consumption

Consumers of the relevant service are sometimes hard to identify (*e.g.* for law and order) Nonetheless they exist in most cases. And they find

   a) supply is *insensitive* to demand, and its changing trends, while being
   b) *oversensitive* to one, some or all of the:
      - relevant political authorities;
      - bureaucracies involved in administering the service;
      - professionals who may actually provide it (teachers, doctors, telephone engineers, etc.).

Production/administration

The phenomena above in *b)* are a typical example of "producer capture". But they are exacerbated by monopoly, which may be a man-made product of law, contract and administration, but will sometimes stem from a real natural monopoly or network. In such circumstances not only is the pressure for efficiency diminished, but so are the stimuli to innovation.

Procurement of assets

The *procurement* process can display a variety of troubling features:

a) The *design-process* can become dominated by technologists, who find the public sector an agreeable, safe place to work made all the more agreeable by the scope it offers to work on vast projects.

b) *Contractors* may learn the value of developing a symbiotic relationship with those procuring assets from them. The consequences are many and varied, but almost always negative.

c) All parties involved find it easy to justify failure cost overruns, inability to meet specifications, delays in completion, etc.

d) Problems of contract design seem to recur again and again. In some cases contractors make obscene profits, or at least appear to do extraordinarily well by supplying "cost plus". In others, they are brought close to disaster by quixotic changes of official policy.

Such phenomena are not new, but they have come to matter more for several reasons. Looking particularly at the years since World War II.

a) Local and central government have, until recently, accepted more and more responsibility for providing services and the infrastructure supporting them.

b) The assets required are no longer relatively simple buildings or structures, at least for the most part. More and more often they are very complex and, often, long-lived; and investment in them now accounts for a much larger share of GDP.

c) Governments now face, almost without exception, acute public spending problems. The large costs, not to mention cost overruns, of infrastructure provision now cause acute embarrassment, whereas decades ago it was much easier to conceal, disregard, explain away or absorb them one way or another.

Why such problems?

Why this state of affairs, in the heart of the most successful and developed market economies? The answers will be blindingly obvious and wearily familiar to those from the CEECs. But they may be less evident to Western experts, some of whom have been telling their opposite numbers in the East how to introduce the market! In sum:

a) No financial market place or prices to give proper effect to consumer demands; and often little or no alternative to the monopoly "product range" offered.

b) Producers not subject to profit and loss disciplines or "hard" budget constraints.

c) Management self-perpetuating and not very accountable to anyone.

d) Stewardship and custody of assets ill-defined, under-developed, and often not even subject to the most basic annual balance sheet treatment.

All in all, these activities are typically part of (or each almost constitutes) a *command economy*. So, although outside the commercial market place, they are in the heart of the *political market place*. These are both recipes for inefficient management.

In such circumstances management is not merely inefficient. The pressures and incentives combine to *confuse roles* or to divide and allocate responsibilities unhelpfully. Risk, uncertainty, success and failure do not provoke or necessitate the explicit techniques and procedures for financial control, risk management, delegation etc. which are standard in commercial organisations.

Such a structural problem has triggered off an interesting sequence of events in countries such as the United Kingdom. As budgetary pressures and rising debt levels become more influential, contact grows between private sector managers and companies and public institutions working on the fringes of the private market. A variety of somewhat inconsistent responses to such pressures and contacts were and are to be seen. Thus:

a) Heavy-spending and politically sensitive public institutions like hospitals fight hard to maintain their right of access to "free" capital, for which they are charged no purchase price, user fee or depreciation. Their response is, naturally, political and defensive of their privileges.

b) Nonetheless, as financial pressures increase, the more cynical and flexible public infrastructure managers may look to the private sector for help. For example leasing assets previously bought outright is a *natural response to budgetary restraint*, one which can subvert Finance Ministry control at a time when the need to tighten it is particularly acute. If such devices are -- as they *can* be -- little more than expensive and blatant ways of escaping financial discipline, then the MOF will in time succeed in imposing *increasingly* ferocious and arbitrary controls. (This certainly happened in the United Kingdom after the IMF "package" of 1976 gave the British Treasury the power it needed to begin to fit locks to every door and bars and armoured glass on every window).

Rigid orthodoxy may help in the short-term by preventing indiscipline. But it reinforces a very undesirable state of affairs in the longer term. The command economy remains supreme within its strongly fortified perimeter. Any scope for public/private partnership, and the private capital it brings, is increasingly ruled out in principle, rather than explored rationally and empirically.

These criticisms can be summed up as inefficiency and the public financing burden. The standard remedy to both -- corporatise and privatise -- is not normally available in what are for the most part non-cash sectors of national life.

Promoting public-private partnership in infrastructure investment

The general remedy sought in recent years in Australia and the United Kingdom is known in the United Kingdom as the "Private Finance Initiative" (PFI) . However, there is nothing intrinsically Anglo-Saxon about it. The principles involved should be of universal interest, not least because their potential applications are both so wide in sectoral coverage and so big, with £5 billion or more of contracts under way in the United Kingdom. The wide ambitions of United Kingdom's PFI initiative are reflected in the requirement imposed a little over a year ago in central government that:

1. *All* central government departments must consider whether their new capital projects can be made "PFI" schemes.

2. The Treasury will only approve public funding for large projects if the PFI financing approach has been proved inadequate.

Annex 1 (Examples of PFI projects in the United Kingdom) outlines a variety of PFI projects in the United Kingdom embracing light railways, roads, prisons, government offices, hospitals, government computing and museums.

Some fundamental principles of the PFI are:

1. The private sector must assume *real* risk, in a given project normally well over 50 per cent.

2. The tax payer's contribution must bring *value-for-money* -- which may be non-financial as well as financial.
   [(1) and (2) are the British Treasury's key tests.]

3. The *risks transferred* to private agents should be those which the private sector handles better: The risks best retained by the public authorities are those in which it excels, usually for the overriding reason that it controls or directly influences them.

4. As a result the public sector buys, not an asset, but a *stream of services* provided by those (privately-owned) assets, on terms specified in a contract with standards, penalties and rewards.

5. Poor service standards will lead to revenue below the minimum which will cover the costs of the private partner; who assumes both *completion* risk on construction, and *performance* risk on operation.

6. "Whole-life costing" becomes a central feature of the contract, *rather than pure capital costs of procurement alone*.

7. The standard description or initials for such contracts are not DBD (Design, Build, Depart) but DBFO: *Design, Build, Finance, Operate*.

Early experience

An approach such as this fairly revolutionary. Thus, for the *public* sector, the emphasis at the start of the project shifts dramatically away from drawing up comprehensive, detailed specifications of *inputs* to defining in the simplest but most precise terms the *outputs*, results, or flow of services sought leaving *competing* contractors to come up with the best answers. This is *not* a welcome change for the many officials and technical specialists who write specifications and control procurement.

For the *private* sector big changes emerge too. Contractors of all kinds, particular suppliers of heavy infrastructure, are under pressure to combine in unfamiliar ways: facilities managers, operating companies, manufacturers, engineers and other consultants -- and, increasingly, financiers. While the new regime will usually offer more work to private companies, the terms are more rigorous, involving demanding explicit treatment of risk, a tight and continuing specification of performance standards with less opportunity for the super-profits contractors used to expect to earn from time to time.

Benefits

These can be discerned in many areas, of which the following are brief examples:

a) *Risk Analysis and clear contracts*

Meticulous risk analysis leads to optimal allocation of responsibilities and control, lower costs and better management. Coupled with it is the key DBFO characteristic of focusing on the quality, and cost of the flow of services provided by the assets over their lifetime; and specification of performance and service quality *e.g.* trains that run on time and remain in sound condition. The traditional procurement framework is far less demanding in both respects, being typically supported by short-lived and limited warranties. In the PFI case the contractor knows from the outset he must support and maintain the assets for their whole lifetime.

b) *Creativity*

A combination of specifying output requirements rather than inputs and a widening of the competitive tendering process, despite the problems alluded to above under *Procurement of assets (b),* can stimulate a wide-range of original ideas from private suppliers.

c) *Shorter construction periods*

Escape from the tight and unpredictable variation of public funding, combined with a greater degree of private project management, permits shorter construction periods and means fewer of the government-induced changes which have bedevilled so many big projects in OECD countries.

d) *Earlier benefits, more intensive use*

Access to private capital is likely to permit projects to be started earlier and successive stages to be initiated more quickly or even at the same time. This brings forward benefits and can increase capacity utilisation in earlier years. However, the contract structures can often stimulate fuller use of assets at all stages.

e) *Economies of scale*

PFI contracts make it possible for private companies to share the advantages of economies of scale. Thus, a "facilities management" company can have one specialist team or organisation to do the job of the separate management teams of several public bodies.

Risk allocation and transfer

The foundation of a PFI-type approach to project funding is thorough risk analysis. Major public infrastructure projects contain risks of many kinds, for example:

Policy Risk: Changes of government, Ministers, policy direction and legislation.

Credit Risk: Failure of public or private partners to meet their obligations.

Administrative Risk: Obtaining planning and environmental permission, satisfying the regulators, meeting safety standards.

Design Risk: Meeting a project specification.

Construction and Maintenance Risk: Constructing and maintaining to specifications of time, price and performance.

Revenue/Demand: Will the usage/traffic levels match those planned/projected/assumed?

Commercial: Will the return be reasonable?

It does not take a genius, nor much time, to note that these risks "belong" more naturally in some places than others. *Thus:*

- political and administrative risks should go to the public sector;
- design and construction risk should lie with the contractor.
- commercial risk should be with the user/operator.
- revenue, demand or traffic risks might best be shared.

As a general rule, the risk should lie with the party or parties which exercise control; and/or which have the requisite skills. If this is done the cost of paying for or assuming a given risk will be minimised and the allocation will be optimised, at least in broad terms. This is therefore a technique for *optimising*, not maximising, the transfer of risk from public to private sectors. Risk analysis of a project may indicate too little risk transfer to permit the project to be deemed private.

Risk analysis is difficult - but possible

Analysing and allocating risks is technically most demanding, and there is little history of it in many parts of the public sector. one project might involve dozens of distinct risks under, say, ten broad headings such as those in the preceding paragraph. The mathematics is nightmarish, even if one can estimate each component risk precisely. *However* decent, second-best, alternative methods have already established. These allow robust judgements about how much of the total risk is transferable, and thus to determine whether the project is fit for private finance; and they make it possible to design proper contract structures.

The risk transfer *must* be "genuine", -- in other words inflict no costs, obligations or liabilities on the public sector in the event of failure, *other than those specified contractually.*

Effect on public spending

When a public body buys an asset, it pays the full price at the outset. With PFI the cost is spread over the lifetime of the asset (or rather the duration of the contract governing its use) . The private partner needs confidence that the relationship will last long enough, which may be ten, twenty years or more. Governments dislike long-term commitments, and their planning horizon is typically four years at most. The expected lifespan of a government (in the strict statistical sense) is rarely over two years. These facts are often paraded by politicians and officials as excuses for keeping partnerships short-term. But they are very bad excuses. Governments can contract over whatever term they like, like other legal persons. And they can build provisions for periodic review, cancellation or early termination into the contract's terms.

Contracts can be devised with a number of distinct and useful features:

a) *Penalties and rewards*

These may be shared above, below, or within certain limits; in constant or differing proportions

b) *Cancellation*

Explicit provision can be made for review, modification of terms, or cancellation; combined with arbitration, alternative dispute resolution etc. This is an obvious way of reassuring investors who are worried about political risk. If pursued systematically, such explicit contracts have the amusing side effect of underlining the costs of policy changes in the conventional public sector -- an embarrassing topic which politicians and officials often prefer not to record, publish or document, let alone discuss.

c) Risk analysis and clear contractual terms for partnerships force all those involved to be much more explicit about risks and uncertainty outside their (or anyone's) control. The proper response will normally be to insure to lay off risk or to build and maintain reserves. The issue of insurance in the public sector raises fascinating further questions which are touched on briefly in *Annex 2.*

Public management, bidding costs, intellectual property rights

Negotiating such contracts is difficult for inexperienced, risk-averse officials. In many countries, it might be better to hire professionals to do the job, at least initially. Amongst other things, officials have a tendency to underestimate the *substantial bidding costs* involved for private groups which enter competitive tenders; and they (or their masters) are prone to change their ideas, terms and conditions in *medias rebus* in a very disruptive way. There are at least two ways of dealing with such problems:

a) the public procurer should offer to pay at least a proportion of the bidder's costs;

b) it might be wise in some cases to choose a preferred contractor at a fairly early stage (probably on the basis of record, financial strength, expertise, etc.) and proceed in a *disciplined* single-tender framework.

The issue of *bidding costs* is one part of the problem of intellectual property rights. Such costs, and the ideas whose development they finance, are likely to be biggest with innovative private companies working in quickly developing sectors, where the scope for big profits and losses is exceptionally large. Such companies will not often want to exhibit their best ideas to governments in "beauty competitions". All too often they find that their services are not used, *but their ideas* are, in a contract which goes to a competitor. Public sector willingness to *pay* for intellectual property rights, even when they are not used, is a partial answer. In the single-tender framework suggested in *b)* above, it would be natural for the public and private partners to share costs almost from the start, and ownership of intellectual property rights arising from the project.

Realism about risks

The public sector in most countries remains reluctant to share risks even when PFI-type activities are well-established. In some cases it would be logical for the public body to subscribe equity, like any other minority investor, even if to do this would seem to involve slipping back into "bad old socialist ways". However, formal creation and public ownership of equity is not always the best or only answer. In some cases what may be required is, rather, a systematic treatment and honest presentation of contingent liabilities. Private Sector standards and procedures for handling such "off-balance sheet" issues are already relatively well developed, and it is time the public sector applied them systematically to itself.

Financial aspects

The discussion hitherto assumes the existence not only of private companies to produce assets and run facilities, but also of a capital market to finance them, to provide both debt and equity. This is unrealistic, at least initially, even in sophisticated OECD economies. In the United Kingdom, it has only been possible to interest the financial markets in *major* PFI projects after a *substantial educational process*, which still has a long way to go. The banks have been willing to provide shorter-term loans from the early stages, at least to smaller projects. But even so, their appetite for longer-term assets is limited. Institutional investors such as life insurance companies and pension funds are more cautious, and need to be introduced carefully to the new philosophy and structures. But since many of their liabilities are very long-term, they are the *classic natural investors* in PFI-type debt, of which much will also be very long-term.

It is also important *not* to expect the infrastructure producers themselves to be major lenders or equity investors at the same time. Such private companies are usually rather undercapitalised, and often operate in sectors with volatile profits. It would only make sense for them to take such risks on a big scale if the returns in prospect are exceptionally big. That said, it gives such companies excellent incentives if they take modest stakes in infrastructure they produce themselves.

Supply of the *external equity* which such projects may need is also an interesting issue. The investment prospects opened up by PFI-type projects differ greatly, ranging from small, highly speculative venture capital stakes (with expected rates of return of as much as 30 per cent) to very large and relatively low risk stakes in projects in which almost everything is certain and settled save the construction process of a project and capacity utilisation thereafter. Sometimes such equity needs might best be met by a new issue on the stock exchange. Others may best be dealt with by specialised intermediaries. Thus in the United Kingdom one of Britain's largest pension organisations has just launched a £100 million private equity fund -- the first in the United Kingdom -- to invest in PFI projects including "transport, health, prisons and other infrastructure traditionally financed by the public sector". If the gearing in such schemes (*i.e.* equity/debt ratio) is low, and a significant proportion of the risk is assumed by the public partner one way or another, then the need for private equity will not, of course, be great.

The most important point to stress, however, is that one should not launch novel policies or arrangements for undertaking projects like privately financed infrastructure, which are financially demanding, without a parallel campaign to stimulate the financial world to play its part.

Table 1. **Alternative ways of organising consumption, production and assets**

Method of consumption	Ownership and control of production/provision	Input and capital assets	Industrial structure
Money	Private	Private	Monopolistic
Direct	Public	Public	Liberal

Table 2. **Classic privatisation of enterprises in the cash economy**

	Consumption method	Ownership and production	Capital assets	Industrial structure
Before privatisation	Money	Public	Public	Liberal/regulated
After privatisation	Money	Private	Private	More liberal

Table 3. **Private finance without privatisation**

	Method of consumption	Control of production	Ownership of assets	Industrial structure
Before privatisation	Direct	Public	Public	Monopoly
After private finance	Direct	Public	Public/private or private	Contestable

Annex 1

A selection of typical projects being undertaken in the UK under the Private Finance Initiative (PFI)

	Contract type	Typical capital value	Typical duration	Progress so far	Examples
Roads	Design, build, finance and operate	£10-200 M	30 years	4 schemes out to tender, 4 more identified	A1-M1 link (new 30 km motorway) A69 (management of 84 km road)
Light rail	Design, build, operate and maintain	£100-200 M	25 years or longer	Schemes at various stages of preparation	Croydon Tramlink, DLR Lewisham Extension
Prisons	Design, construct, maintain and finance	£70M	25 years	2 schemes out to tender, 4 more planned	Bridgend and Fazakerley (Merseyside)
Office Accommodation	Developer granted long term interest in land. Public sector commits to initial period	Various up to £200M	15 years or less	Some major schemes identified with preparation underway	DSS Newcastle Estate Treasury Refurbishment
Museum	Developer granted interest in land in return for construction and operation	£20M (Science Museum)	Various	1 scheme currently out to render	Science Museum
District General Hospital	Design, build, maintain and operate non clinical services	£40-90M	25 years?	5 schemes advertised	Carlisle Hospital, Norfolk and Norwich Hospital
Urban Regeneration	Public asset contribution to company controlled by private sector	£5M	Not transferred back	Many schemes around the country	Docklands Exhibition Centre, Bristol Harbourside
Information Technology	Supply and maintenance (and operation) of equipment and system software.	£5-500M	5 - 10 years	2 major projects currently out to tender. Many others in preparation	National Insurance Recording System NRS 2

Source: Local Authorities and the Private Finance Initiative, a consultation paper by the Private Finance Panel.

Note on Insurance and Capital Charging

Insurance

In public sector circles in the West insurance is often dismissed as suitable only for private persons and organisations. Common reasons include:

a) The public sector is so big that the "law of large numbers" eliminates the need to insure.

b) Why pay outside (presumably private) entities a premium and a profit margin to receive something which the public sector can provide more economically itself?

Such views are complacent, and often wrong. While the large size of "the public sector" does smooth the impact of shocks and provide stability, that is not an argument for doing nothing. The case for identifying specific risks measuring and pricing them in some sense is *unrelated* to the size of organisation. It is the right micro-economic strategy under *any* circumstances. However the size of and relationship between the constituents of an organisation are major considerations in determining whether to self-insure or to insure with an outside organisation. Whichever of those routes is followed, size and internal structure will affect the premium charged for given risks, and the reserving levels needed by the insurer for them.

Charging for capital

Consideration of pricing risk leads directly to the issue of charging for capital. In a market economy, private entities pay for the capital they secure externally; and public quoted companies have to justify their performance to the capital markets. In addition, use of capital is often priced internally within complex companies. The "price" of such capital will embody a risk premium appropriate to the riskiness of the sector, activity or project. That premium is conceptually a supplement to the *risk-free rate of return*. In some parts of the public sector in the United Kingdom and in many other countries, there is (or has till recently been) *no* charge for capital use as such. Investment *appraisals* have long been required in the United Kingdom, with test discount rates. But usually the rate set by the Treasury is low-risk; and there has typically been no charge levied for capital supplied by the Treasury, or even comparison of the actual return of capital with the estimates made when a project is launched. In such conditions capital obtained internally in the budgeting process is *free* when you can get it; and hence infinitely preferable to (private)capital which has a real cost, even if that private capital is usually available while public funds are harder to obtain.

Introducing the possibility of private finance for public projects therefore calls for the famous "level playing field" if potentially desirable privately funded projects are to be compared properly with publicly financed alternatives. This may seen obvious or trivial. But such capital charging is often forgotten in activities which are far from the market, like hospitals, prisons or military installations. Introducing charges in such areas can be almost revolutionary!

Once capital charging is introduced, yet another vision opens up. You cannot charge for the use of capital without establishing its value. It may seem self-evident that such information should be compiled regularly in an annual balance sheet for every serious public agency in any OECD country. In fact, such balance sheets are not compiled regularly or, in many countries and sectors, at all. The notable exception, the pioneers in this, as so much else, are to be found in New Zealand.

In the United Kingdom major moves of this kind have been initiated in recent years to introduce what is known as "Resource Accounting". These are set on in the Government's Green Paper *Better Accounting for the Taxpayers' Money: Resource Accounting and Budgeting in Government*. 13 July 1994, Cmnd 2626; and the White Paper under the same title of 26 July 1995, Cmnd 2929.

ISSUES OF CONTRACTUAL DESIGN IN THE CONTEXT OF PRIVATE PARTICIPATION IN INFRASTRUCTURE PROJECTS

*Douglas Webb**

Introduction

New investment in infrastructure in developing countries represents four per cent of their national output and a fifth of their total investment: that is, some US$ 200 billion a year.[1] By 2025 more than two-thirds of the developing world's population will live in cities, with consequently rapidly-increasing demands for urban services such as transportation, access to safe water supplies and adequate solid waste management.[2]

Many countries are increasingly turning to the private sector[3] for the provision of infrastructure through contractual mechanisms ranging from management contracts and build-operate-transfer (BOT) and build-operate-own (BOO) arrangements through to full private ownership of new infrastructure facilities.[4] Among the reasons for this trend are:

i) limited budgetary resources to meet the massive financial demands for new investment in infrastructure;

ii) reluctance or inability to obtain financing through further sovereign borrowings or from other sources (*e.g.* domestic or international capital markets);

iii) the need to obtain technological and operational know-how; and

iv) a recognition that private participation can bring new efficiencies and in addition reduce or avoid adverse environmental and health effects.

The debt financing required for large-scale infrastructure projects in developing countries is, however, in limited supply because the appetite of lenders is constrained by the significant political or country risks which often exist in such projects as well as the long-term nature of the loans required in order to match the lengthy amortisation of project assets.

This paper examines the characteristics of a contractually-driven relationship between the state and a private operator of infrastructure, and considers the linkage between such contracts and the wider legal and institutional setting. The analysis of contractual mechanisms is set in the context of the general pattern of risk allocation in typical non-recourse or limited-recourse project financings.

---

* This paper was presented by Douglas Webb, Legal Advisor, Legal Reform and Private Sector Development Unit, at the eighth meeting of the Advisory Group on Privatisation "Privatisation of Utilities and Infrastructure: Methods and Constraints", held in Paris, 30 and 31 October 1995. The views expressed in this article are those of the author and should not be attributed to the World Bank.

The paper describes the mechanisms used by the World Bank Group to reduce some of the key risks which deter private sector participation in infrastructure and notes the wider relationship between the commercial and political risks assumed respectively by the various private sector parties, the host government, national export credit agencies, the World Bank and other members of the World Bank Group (IFC and MIGA).

The role of contracts

The privatisation of business assets in markets which are competitive or have low barriers to the entry of new participants relies upon market forces to ensure that those assets will be used efficiently.[5] With the exception of undertakings provided by the buyer as to the continuity of the existing line of business, or as to investment or the maintenance of employment levels, the state relies upon general legislation (such as competition law) to protect the public interest in the manner in which the privately-owned business is conducted.

Where the asset to be disposed of is either the physical asset used to provide infrastructure services (such as a telecommunications network or a rail system) or the intangible right to set up a "greenfield" infrastructure project, the state will have a continuing interest in adjusting for the "market failure" characteristic of such monopolistic activities. In particular, the state will wish to ensure that universal service is provided to all citizens where the private operator deals directly with individual citizens as the consumers of the service, that the service is provided to an adequate standard, and that tariffs provide an adequate but not excessive return.

The expression of this continuing relationship can be in the form of a specific law or regulation. In that event, the rules are uniform for all cases, they are publicly known, and potential private investors have the comfort of knowing that changes to the rules will, depending on the nature of the legislative process, be infrequent. In circumstances where there are likely to be multiple private providers and a stable technology or service delivery type, such legislation provides a high degree of transparency and certainty.[6] And the use of legislation may also minimise the enforcement risk inherent in the contractual alternative, particularly where the judicial system is unreliable.

The same characteristics of stability and predictability are, however, potential disadvantages where the service is predominantly monopolistic, and flexibility is essential to incentivise private operators to continually drive down costs and adopt new technologies. Individually designed contracts[7] allow for the specification of detailed service obligations, performance and investment targets, tariffing regimes, and obligations to permit new entrants to interconnect with a fixed network, while allowing for periodic reviews either at the initiative of the private operator or the state if there has been a material change in country or sector conditions. In this sense, a contract-based infrastructure service is tailored to the needs of an individual project or geographic area[8] and embodies an individual regulatory regime.

In addition to the flexibility provided by the ability to design specific contractual terms, the bidding process for the right to provide a contract-based infrastructure service allows the private sector to use the bidding process as a means of testing the marketability of the contractual terms and to propose alternative means of meeting the government's objectives in a more efficient manner.

The preceding discussion has focused on the "upstream" contract by which a private operator is granted the right either to use state-owned assets, or to acquire or create privately-owned facilities, to provide an infrastructure service. However, private provision of infrastructure services typically also involves "downstream" contracts with other state entities, either as the providers of inputs or the buyers of outputs. Those contracts will be normal arms-length commercial arrangements and will not differ from those entered into in similar circumstances between two private parties.

The contractual framework as a disciplining force

The preparation and negotiation of the contractual arrangements for private participation in infrastructure has a disciplining effect on a host government in that it requires the government:

i) to identify precisely what services it requires and what inputs and undertakings it is prepared to provide in return;

ii) to accept restraints on its freedom of action, especially in regard to the pricing of public services;

iii) to establish a mechanism for monitoring performance by the private operator;[9] and

iv) to submit to a contractual dispute resolution mechanism.

The acceptance by a government of these constraints and adherence to them can enable a government to build up credibility and establish a "track record" which will encourage further private sector investment.

The converse is also true however. Failure by a government to adhere to its contractual commitments, if unchecked by the judicial system, can rapidly erode private sector confidence in the integrity of the contractual process. Given the political sensitivity of infrastructure tariff levels in many developing countries, governments may face strong public pressures to roll back tariff increases regardless of contractual provisions allowing the private operator to impose those increases.[10]

Identifying the contracting party

The shift from state provision to private provision of infrastructure requires the substitution of a contractual matrix for the poorly defined service obligations typical of state-owned operators. The design of that contractual matrix starts with the identification of all the separate elements required for service delivery, whether those elements are in the form of inputs (fuel oil, gas, etc.), permissions (*e.g.* rights of access to the existing infrastructure network in order to perform the service) or promises as to the purchase of outputs by other state entities (*e.g.* take-or-pay contracts for electric power supplied by a private generator to a state-owned distributor).

Once those elements have been identified, the next stage is to allocate responsibilities for contractual performance to the appropriate state agencies. Often those state agencies in turn may face pressure to restructure themselves in order to ensure their capacity to perform their new obligations under an arms-length contract with a private operator. In addition, the need to price the inputs to be provided to the private operator will focus attention on identifying the costs of that provision, in order to avoid an unintended subsidy to the private operator or the inefficient use of resources, and to enable the government to assess pricing proposals made by private operators during the tender process.

Resolving disputes

The use of contractual mechanisms to support private provision of infrastructure necessarily implies that the contractual terms will be paramount and that those terms will not be altered unilaterally by the government.[11] Private investment in infrastructure typically takes the form of large investments with low alternative, or salvage, value. If those investments are not sheltered by a reliable system of enforceable contracts, private investors are likely to invest inadequate amounts, factor a high risk premium into the tariff structure, or refrain from investing at all.[12]

The legal system must therefore be capable of:

a) restraining administrative actions by officials which are inconsistent with government's contractual obligations; and

b) resolving promptly and fairly disputes arising between the parties to the contract as to its interpretation and implementation.

If the courts are competent and free from political interference, private investors will be willing to invest in reliance on their commercial judgments as to likely outcomes in the area of demand, pricing, and stability of revenue flows.

Conversely, where the courts are less effective in protecting and enforcing contractual rights, private investors will wish to shift key government obligations into legislation, which may be more immune to unilateral changes.

Even the alternative of third-party arbitration, such as through the International Chamber of Commerce, may be insufficient comfort where domestic courts are still essential in order to recognise and enforce the resulting arbitral awards.

The use of guarantees of non-commercial risk (discussed later) may, however, lend credibility to contractual undertakings by government entities.

Risk allocation

Private participation in infrastructure requires that the risks assumed by the private sector parties (*e.g.* project sponsors, senior lenders, construction contractors, equipment suppliers) and the host government must be clearly defined in the relevant contracts.

The overriding principle is that each type of risk should rest with the party best able to control it. Accordingly, commercial risks relating to the design, construction and the availability of financing are best handled by the private sector whereas political risks should rest with the host government.

As between the private sector parties to an infrastructure project, this will mean that:

i) completion risk (*i.e.* the risk that the project will not be completed within the agreed time and price) will rest with the construction contractor subject to a fixed price, firm date, turnkey construction contract with stipulated liquidated damages, often supplemented by performance bonds;

ii) performance and operating risk (*i.e.* that the project will not perform as expected) will be covered by warranties from the construction contractors and equipment suppliers and performance guarantees from the operator/maintainer;

iii) destruction of plant and equipment (and other insurable risks) could be covered by casualty insurance, third party liability insurance, workmen's compensation insurance, etc.

The host government will in turn provide guarantees[13] or other undertakings in the concession or through special legislation relating to those areas of risk over which the private sector parties have little or no control. The primary political or country risks are:

i) purchase risks through off-take agreements where a state-owned utility is the sole purchaser of the service provided by the private producer;

ii) supply risks where a state-owned entity is the sole supplier of fuel or other inputs required by the project company;

iii) inflation risks, which can be mitigated by a suitable inflation-linked price escalation clause in the case of a bulk supply agreement or an inflation-linked tariff cap in the concession agreement in the case of a private utility;

iv) foreign exchange risks, including the risk of non-convertibility of local currency earnings into foreign currency, of insufficient foreign currency or an adverse conversion rate at the time of conversion, to be mitigated either by a government guarantee through the central bank of foreign currency availability or by placing an obligation on the state-owned purchasing utility to make periodic payments under the off-take contract in a basket of blue-chip currencies to match the payments required to be made to the foreign lenders and investors; and

v) political force majeure events causing delay in the construction or interruption in the operation of the project.

The host government will, in certain circumstances, also provide some of the financing for the project,[14] whether debt, equity or even on a standby subordinated loan basis. For example, in the context of a toll road project, the senior lenders may insist that the host government agree to provide subordinated loans to the project company whenever toll revenues fall below a certain minimum.

Political risk minimisation is designed to neutralise non-commercial impacts on the revenue stream. Classical political risks are not project-specific but arise from macroeconomic policies pursued by government. The risks of non-performance by state entities or lack of market demand are project-specific though classical political risks may in turn be causative. Performance or market risks vary depending upon the type of infrastructure project and the primary revenue sources, whether:

i) a single state-owned entity (e.g. a state-owned purchaser in the case of a power generating plant);

ii) state-owned and private end-users (e.g. airlines in the case of an airport, shipping companies in the case of a port facility, interconnecting network operators in the case of certain telecommunications projects);

iii) individual citizens (e.g. road users in the case of a toll road; subscribers in the case of a telecommunications project).

Indirectly, the use of a BOT (as opposed to a BOO) arrangement provides private sector parties with some general measure of assurance since the transfer element of the BOT arrangement should to some extent serve as a disincentive for the government to take action which would prejudice the ultimate success and transfer of the project.

Private sector participants in infrastructure projects will often obtain insurance or guarantees from their own export credit agencies, MIGA and/or the IFC. The coverage provided by these entities will, however, be limited in scope.

MIGA guarantees, for example, typically cover the "standard" sovereign risks of foreign exchange, war, civil disturbance and expropriation. Further, MIGA is currently subject to a limit of US$50 million per project and US$150 million of outstanding guarantees per country.

The IFC currently provides equity and debt financing on its own account and debt financing from commercial sources under its B-loan syndication umbrella. The latter provides comfort against foreign exchange risks but not against the other forms of governmental performance failure.

World Bank guarantees

Since September 1994, the World Bank has provided both partial risk and partial credit guarantees as a normal instrument of Bank operations (rather than, as had hitherto been the case, solely as a cofinancing instrument), particularly as a mechanism to promote private sector participation in infrastructure projects.

In the context of large-scale infrastructure projects, the partial risk and partial credit guarantees can, respectively, be used as mechanisms for allaying private sector concerns over political risk and the long maturity periods typically required of loans for non-recourse or limited-recourse infrastructure projects.

The partial risk guarantee is designed to overcome private sector concerns about lending to a project because of political risks associated with that project. Partial risk guarantees (as deployed for example in the Pakistan Hub River Project and the Jamaica Rockfort Power Project) can be used to mitigate against specific political risks.

A partial risk guarantee could, for example, apply to certain of the political risks in respect of which host government undertakings had been given to private sector parties. It is important to note, however, that a partial risk guarantee would only be triggered to the extent that non-compliance by the host government with such an undertaking under the project agreements resulted in debt service default to lenders.

World Bank partial risk guarantees have two additional attractions for private sector participants in infrastructure projects. First, the World Bank's Articles of Agreement require that (as with World Bank loans) the Bank obtain a counter-guarantee from the borrower for the Bank guarantee. The counter-guarantee is normally in the form of an indemnity agreement whereby the government agrees to indemnify the Bank in respect of any payments made by the Bank under its guarantee.

A practical effect of the counter-guarantee is, therefore, that it demonstrates commitment on the part of the host government (over and above any obligations assumed by the host government under the project agreements) to meet its contractual obligations to the private parties.

The second attraction flows from the traditional "honest broker" role of the Bank, through its lending and guarantee operations, in advising its borrower governments about realistic policy frameworks for the sector in question and the type of government initiatives necessary in order to promote private sector investment.

The Bank's presence is seen by investors as a stabilising factor, not only because of the political risks covered by the Bank guarantee, but also because of the Bank's long-standing relationship with governments, project appraisal and supervision capacity and ability to address surrounding issues concerning the viability of the business environment.

The differentiation of political and commercial risks and the need to draw a "bright line" between them is likely to be an ongoing issue for the providers of non-domestic guarantees. International financial institutions such as the World Bank will wish to use their finite appetite for guarantees in order to underwrite only those risks which either could not be borne by the private sector or could only be borne at a disproportionate cost.

In the case of a toll road project, for instance, the project sponsors might seek assurances as to a minimum revenue stream based on an assumed minimum number of road users. The experience of Mexico, a pioneer in the granting of concessions for private toll roads, has been that future traffic projections can be extremely unreliable, and as a consequence, a number of private roads have proven not to be viable. Surprisingly, such experiences have not had a chilling effect on the ability of governments to privatise roading projects other than those on major traffic corridors with significant undercapacity. Yet it is doubtful whether IFI guarantees will be available to underwrite future government guarantees of toll revenues, notwithstanding the difficulty of attracting significant private investment without them.

Another key issue is the balance to be struck between enhancing the viability of a large scale infrastructure project by supporting project sponsor requirements for exclusivity and the adoption of a general policy for the sector which encourages the competitive provision of services through entry liberalisation. The Bank would probably be unwilling to provide a guarantee in relation to a contractual undertaking to prevent the entry of future competitors.

Under a partial credit guarantee, the World Bank assumes the repayment risk for a limited time. The purpose of the guarantee is to improve the borrowing terms for the private project sponsors by lengthening the maturity of the loan and therefore addressing the concerns of lenders as to the long-term maturity periods of infrastructure loans.

A partial credit guarantee can, for example, be structured so as to help transform available medium-term financing into longer-term financing by providing for:

i) longer-date maturities in a similar way to the IFC's B-loan program;

ii) providing incentives for lenders to roll over their medium term loans at maturity;

iii) providing liquidity guarantees in the form of put-options and take-out financing (for example post-construction);

iv) rolling guarantees that cover a fixed number of scheduled payments.

The World Bank's partial risk and partial credit guarantees only apply to lenders to an infrastructure project, since the Bank does not have the authority to guarantee equity investments (although MIGA and national export credit agencies can provide coverage for equity).

However, the provision by the World Bank of a guarantee in the context of a non-recourse or limited-recourse infrastructure project will generally provide comfort to other categories of investors with concerns similar to those of the lenders. This can result in a significant leverage effect.

The Bank will only provide credit enhancement by way of guarantees in relation to infrastructure projects that otherwise would not go ahead with financing or guarantees from other sources, for example, MIGA, IFC, national export credit agencies.

Finally, World Bank guarantees can operate as a transitional means for a developing country to build up credibility and a track record in relation to private sector investment pending establishment of a stable, comprehensive, legal and regulatory framework. This is similar to the way in which reliance on bespoke contractual arrangements can operate as a transitional substitute for a comprehensive legal and regulatory sector framework.

Infrastructure investment funds

In addition to mainstreaming guarantees as a means of promoting private participation in infrastructure, the World Bank is placing increasing emphasis on the use of infrastructure investment funds.

There are, essentially, two types of infrastructure investment funds: private infrastructure funds and government-sponsored infrastructure investment funds. Both share the objective of catalysing private sector investment in infrastructure. Within the World Bank Group, the IFC has played an important role in establishing private infrastructure funds while the World Bank has played a key role in the establishment of government-sponsored funds.

Private infrastructure investment funds are essentially equity funds whose main objective is to achieve long-term capital appreciation through investing in equity or quasi-equity of infrastructure companies/projects in emerging markets.

The government-sponsored funds which the World Bank has been instrumental in establishing (in particular, the Private Sector Energy Development Fund in Pakistan and the Private Sector Energy Fund in Jamaica) are designed to provide long-term loans to private project sponsors.

What distinguishes these funds from traditional government infrastructure funds is their market orientation in terms, for example, of:

i) providing loans to project sponsors at interest rates that reflect the true market cost of long-term capital;

ii) private or quasi-private management, even though the fund is established under the jurisdiction of a government agency.

Conclusion

Infrastructure projects possess several characteristics which lend themselves to the use of binding contracts as the vehicle for allocating risks and assigning responsibilities between the state and a private investor or operator. Such projects typically involve the production and delivery of a generic service (electric power; telecommunications; road access; water supply and waste removal) to large numbers of users who themselves have little or no bargaining power in their dealings with the infrastructure provider. The investment costs are often large relative to the domestic economy and the resultant assets have little salvage value.

In these circumstances, the state has a responsibility to define universal service standards in order to ensure that all members of society have access to the public goods represented by the output of the infrastructure operator. And a mechanism must be adopted to permit tariff setting in a politically neutral environment so that the operator can achieve an adequate, but not unreasonable, profit and is thereby encouraged to make further investments in improving service quality and availability.

The contractual form provides a means of achieving these goals while permitting flexibility to tailor the terms to the needs of the specific sector, project, and even investor.

Private provision of infrastructure is typically embedded into a range of commercial relationships with a variety of state entities, including regulatory bodies, state-owned utilities, and state-owned suppliers of essential inputs. The preparation and negotiation of a bankable contractual structure may therefore impose on the government the necessity to unbundle these relationships and to sharpen its focus on the precise nature of the infrastructure services to be provided, and the efficient delivery of inputs and other complementary services to be provided by state entities.

The allocation of risks is a further dimension of contractual design. Both political and commercial risks must be accurately identified and assumed by the party best able to control those risks. To the extent that political or country risks represent the risk of default by a state entity, the government may agree to provide a performance guarantee. In doing so, the government should pursue reforms in order that in the longer-term the default risk is minimised.

The World Bank can provide guarantees of a variety of country risks in circumstances where a direct government guarantee provides insufficient comfort. In addition, partial credit guarantees assist in lengthening the maturity of loans available to the project sponsors.

Governments may also be required to fill a funding gap by providing long-term loans through infrastructure investment funds established for the purpose.

The marriage of the contractual form with wider sector reform offers the prospect of increased efficiency within the public sector, as well as improvement in the quality and accessibility of infrastructure services provided by the private sector.

Notes

1. See World Bank, *1994 World Development Report* at page 1. The 1994 World Development Report refers to developing countries as low-income countries (with a GNP per capita of US$675 or less in 1992) and middle-income countries (with a GNP per capita of more than US$675 but less than US$8 356 in 1992).

2. *The Business of Sustainable Cities: Public - Private Partnerships for Creative, Technical and Institutional Solutions*, World Bank 1995.

3. For countries belonging to the administrative law tradition, the contracting-out of public services through concessions has a long history. The government retains its legal prerogative to provide the service, while delegating the function to a private or public/private operator.

4. Because of the monopolistic character of most infrastructure provision, the right to provide infrastructure services is typically granted by the state or a municipality in the form of a license or concession. In addition, if the buyer of those services is another state entity such as a power distributor, the commercial terms of that relationship will be embodied in one or several contracts (for example, contracts requiring the bulk purchaser to take a fixed minimum quantity of output at a pre-determined price or to pay an equivalent sum in lieu).

5. If not by the original buyer, then by a subsequent buyer.

6. Private operators will often be granted a license or other form of revocable right to provide the service subject to continued compliance with the service standards set in the law.

7. The procedures to be followed for the award of the contract and basic parameters such as the length of any exclusivity may be prescribed by a general law such as the Philippines BOT Law.

8. Most infrastructure concessions in France are granted by municipalities and are local in character.

9. In Bogota, Columbia, the municipality has hired a private firm to monitor the performance of several private companies providing refuse collection.

10. Recent instances of government intervention to prevent price adjustments include: the Tenaga National Electricity Utility (Malaysia); and the Bangkok Expressway Project (Thailand). The cancellation of the Enron Dahbol Project in India was at least in part motivated by concerns as to the pre-agreed tariff levels for power to be generated under the project.

11. The state retains the power to alter the contractual arrangements by legislation, but any such alteration should not increase the obligations of the private operator or reduce those of the state.

12. Though increasingly Central and Eastern European foreign investment laws permit third-party arbitration of contractual disputes.

13. Though blanket government guarantees should be seen as an interim measure pending the emergence of commercially viable private markets for infrastructure services, accompanied by stable and independent regulatory mechanisms.

14. See the discussion (following) of government-sponsored infrastructure funds.

PRIVATE SECTOR INVESTMENT IN INFRASTRUCTURE PROJECTS: THE CASE OF VICTORIA

Peter Noble[*]

1. Victoria, Australia

Victoria is one of the six states and two territories that form the Commonwealth of Australia. The State of Victoria is located in the south eastern part of the country, occupying land approximately the size of Britain.

Victoria has the highest population density, with 25 per cent of the national population (4.5 million people) living on three per cent of the continent. It is the second most populous state after New South Wales.

Melbourne is the state's capital city and has a population of approximately three million which is almost 70 per cent of the total population of Victoria. Melbourne was determined one of the world's most liveable cities in 1990 by Populations Crisis Committee, a research group based in Washington, USA.

Politics

Australia is a parliamentary democracy with a federal system of government. The Commonwealth constitution prescribes the powers of the Commonwealth government. Some of these are held concurrently with the states. The Commonwealth is responsible for international relations, trade and defence services, whereas the States have control over health, education, transport, the justice system, natural resources and energy.

A third system of government exists that provides municipal services. Local Councils manage issues at a smaller scale, such as land use planning, local roads, traffic control, health regulations, garbage collection and welfare and recreation services.

Taxation in Australia is collected substantially by the Commonwealth. State and local governments have access to limited sources of taxation revenue.

---

[*] This paper was presented by Peter Noble, Director, Project and Outsourcing Development, Department of Treasury, Australia, at the eighth meeting of the Advisory Group on Privatisation "Privatisation of Utilities and Infrastructure: Methods and Constraints", held in Paris, 30 and 31 October 1995.

Taxation is a significant issue in private investment in infrastructure. The states are not liable to pay Commonwealth taxes when providing infrastructure. However, a private firm engaged to provide infrastructure in the place of the state would be liable for Commonwealth company tax.

Economy

In 1994-95 Victoria's Gross State Product (GSP) was Australian dollars (A$) 120 billion, 26 per cent of the national Gross Domestic Product (GDP). During that same year the State produced 32 per cent of total manufacturing output, 25 per cent of agricultural output and 24 per cent of agricultural export earnings.

Manufacturing accounts for 18 per cent of GSP and employment in the state. Retail and wholesale industries account for 14 per cent of GSP and employ 21 per cent of the workforce. Public administration, health, welfare and defence services contribute 18 per cent of GSP.

2. Winds of change

For most of this century at least, infrastructure provision in Australia has been almost exclusively the preserve of government, particularly of state governments.

Traditionally, Australian governments have provided, for example, almost all of the nation's transport, electricity, gas and water infrastructure and services and the great majority of education and health infrastructure and services.

By the early 1990's, however, a change was occurring and state governments sought to promote privately financed projects.

Similarly, the Australian federal government, whose role in direct provision of infrastructure is largely limited to airports, defence, telecommunications and some tertiary education, is now seeking to transfer to the private sector greater responsibility for ownership and operation of infrastructure.

The reasons for the willingness of governments to change their approach are complex, but economic and financial necessity and a fundamental shift in political outlook are dominant influences.

The economic forces driving the change at state level were:

− on the one hand, a real limit to the extent that state governments could fund new or improved infrastructure, particularly in an environment of relatively static revenues and high accumulated debt; and on the other, a continuing growth in demand for economic and social infrastructure by both the business community and the public in general;

− constitutional limitations on the capacity of Australian states to raise additional taxation revenue;

− successive real reductions in the value of grants received from the federal government;

− an increase in the proportion of total grants from the federal government which were tied to specific purposes and therefore not available for general purpose expenditure; and

– changes to funding arrangements by the Australian Loan Council which restricted state borrowing opportunities.

In Victoria, the pressure to supplement scarce public dollars was particularly evident. Over the decade to 1991-92, Victorian government expenditure on new fixed assets had fallen by 47 per cent with real per capita expenditure on new fixed assets falling well below that of other states. By moving a project into the private sector, the government recognised that it would be able to bring forward needed investment and free up its limited financial resources to meet other high priority funding requirements.

Accompanying the view of an expanded role for the private sector was an emerging recognition that there is a distinction between the role of the planner and regulator (a role suited to governments) and the role of the owner and operator (a role more suited to the private and community sectors). Public administrators are now exhorted to "steer" not "row", a theme that was articulated in works such as *Reinventing Government*", (1992) by David Osborne and Ted Gaebler.

Australian governments have also come to recognise that there are benefits to be gained by the application, within a competitive market, of private sector skills in design, construction, operation, financing, maintenance and from private sector commercial and innovative customer-responsive management in general.

From its attainment of office in October 1992, the current Victorian government has actively been pursuing private investment in infrastructure and service delivery. The Victorian government is now prominent in this field in Australia.

Additionally, all Australian governments have now adopted a consistent national approach to Competition Policy, including the principle of competitive neutrality. Government-owned businesses are now expected to compete with private sector businesses on the same footing. Victoria has in train a major program of reform of public monopolies to introduce competition into key energy, water and transport infrastructure service industries through corporatisation and privatisation. While the privatisation program is being undertaken principally to enhance competitive outcomes in the Victorian economy, the proceeds will have a significant impact on reducing the State debt.

3.   Infrastructure investment policy for Victoria

Over the past three years, a range of investment opportunities for business has been opened up in a variety of Victorian government portfolios, including opportunities to build and operate facilities such as prisons and roads; privatisation of activities such as energy supply; and contracting out of activities such as information technology.

Victorian government policy is that private enterprise is to be actively encouraged to invest in the State's future wherever benefits in terms of efficiency and cost effectiveness can be demonstrated.

The *Infrastructure Investment Policy for Victoria ("the Policy")*, released in August 1994, demonstrates the government's commitment to strengthening its partnership with the private sector.

Policy objectives

The *Policy* has the purpose of assisting Victorian government agencies and private proponents seeking investment in State infrastructure, facilities and services.

The *Policy* sets out clear and concise guidelines, promoting greater certainty for business in making infrastructure investment decisions.

The government is pursuing a number of objectives:

- to procure assets, goods and services in the most efficient, cost-effective and timely manner;

- to take advantage of new technologies and innovations, private sector management skills and a wide range of financing techniques;

- to promote the growth of new and existing Victorian businesses and employment; and

- to strengthen the state's economy, producing sustainable social, cultural and other quality of life benefits.

Issues addressed

The *Policy* addresses a range of significant aspects of private enterprise involvement in the financing and provision of public infrastructure, including: setting out principles for assessing the merits of proposals for private sector investment; examples of appropriate forms of investment; the process to be adopted in developing infrastructure projects with the private sector; and provisions to apply to intellectual property and confidentiality.

It demonstrates an ongoing government commitment to reducing uncertainties faced by the private sector in pursuing project opportunities, while increasing efficiency of the bidding process and minimising costs to the private sector.

The *Policy* encourages competitive bidding and allocation of risk to those parties best positioned to assess and manage it, providing rewards for enterprise and risk-taking through appropriate returns within a competitive environment whilst securing benefits for the Victorian community.

Importantly, project briefs aim to minimise specification of the means of meeting requirements and instead focus as far as possible on specification of the end goods or services sought or, more broadly, on the need to be addressed. Thus private proponents are challenged to provide creative solutions to service delivery needs.

Forms of private involvement

Private sector investment is encouraged in both new and existing infrastructure and services.

The *Policy* applies to all projects including contracting out activities, with a total project value in excess of A$ 10 million, undertaken on behalf of the Victorian government, including its agencies, and which involve private sector investment or financing.

Areas of private sector involvement include operating and management contracts, turnkey project delivery, build-operate-transfer projects and build-own-operate projects, or privatisation within such industries as energy, health, water and sewerage.

While the government is not committed to any one form of private sector participation, there is an overriding requirement to ensure that a project can be structured to achieve ongoing benefit to both the private sector and the government.

Project management

Each project is allocated to a responsible government minister, generally the minister with portfolio responsibility for the need that is serviced by the project.

However, the Victorian Treasurer's particular responsibilities require that the Treasurer work with the responsible minister in determining the financial and commercial aspects.

Project development is undertaken by a Management Panel, supported by a Project Team. While the Management Panel of necessity must include representatives of the responsible government department and the Department of Treasury and Finance, the make up of membership otherwise will vary from project to project. Generally, the field of expertise covered by members will include:

- capacity to identify and assess critical factors in the design, delivery and operation of the particular type of infrastructure, including a good comprehension of the inherent risks;
- capacity to structure robust commercial relationships appropriate to the type of business; and
- capacity to analyse financial structures, including their dependence on particular taxation rulings and their sensitivity to monetary and fiscal policy developments or other external factors.

In almost all circumstances the Management Panel comprises a mix of experienced public and private sector people. Having the right people in this steering role is of crucial importance on a significantly sized project.

The Project Team generally also has a mix of experts from the responsible department and from other areas of government, together with a range of specialist consultants. Consultants may be engaged as full time members of a Team or may be retained to participate when particular skills are needed.

A key appointment is that of Project Director, the person who will live with the project through the months of development and who may be the major influence on the degree of success of the project.

The process of project management and project approval, including the roles of the Responsible Department, the Management Panel and the Government, are summarised below.

Process summary

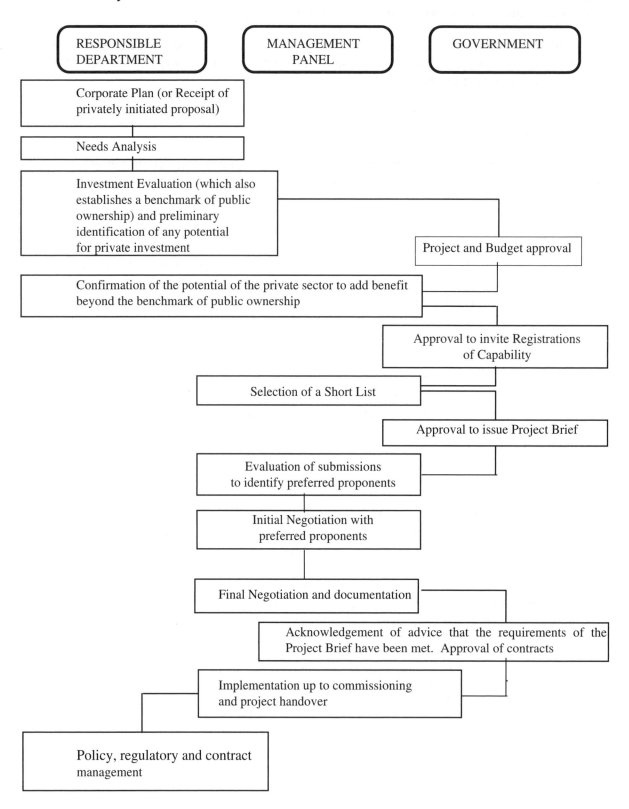

RESPONSIBLE DEPARTMENT

MANAGEMENT PANEL

GOVERNMENT

Corporate Plan (or Receipt of privately initiated proposal)

Needs Analysis

Investment Evaluation (which also establishes a benchmark of public ownership) and preliminary identification of any potential for private investment

Project and Budget approval

Confirmation of the potential of the private sector to add benefit beyond the benchmark of public ownership

Approval to invite Registrations of Capability

Selection of a Short List

Approval to issue Project Brief

Evaluation of submissions to identify preferred proponents

Initial Negotiation with preferred proponents

Final Negotiation and documentation

Acknowledgement of advice that the requirements of the Project Brief have been met. Approval of contracts

Implementation up to commissioning and project handover

Policy, regulatory and contract management

Approval process

A major concern for private sector parties, addressed by the *Policy*, is the incidence in Australia, as in other countries, of cancellation or radical change to projects on which considerable sums have been spent by bidders in research and preparation of bids.

A three-stage government approval process involves:

− approval by government to call for Registrations of Capability;
− approval by government to issue a detailed Project Brief;
− approval by the Responsible Minister and the Treasurer of proposed contracts as properly conforming with the previous project approvals, and a report to government confirming that the requirements of the project brief have been met by a bidder and hence that the project may proceed.

Prior to giving approval to call for Registrations of Capability, the government requires a reliable assessment that the private sector can potentially provide a benefit to a project.

A firm demonstration of project viability is then required before approving the issue of a detailed Project Brief.

The government intends that once the Project Brief has been issued a project will proceed to implementation, subject only to achievement of the functional and other requirements specified in the Project Brief, including any cost to government.

Risk management

It is recognised that a successful negotiation of contracts relies on a common understanding of risk identification and quantification, and on an appropriate risk allocation profile being established between the parties.

Identified risks are allocated to those parties best positioned to assess and manage them. It is expected that the majority of risks, particularly risks associated with the design, construction, financing and operation of an asset, will be borne by the private sector.

Intellectual property

The *Policy* ensures that intellectual and commercial property of private sector proponents is adequately protected against leakage to competitors or illegitimate use by public sector agencies.

To maximise the scope for competitive bidding, the government may negotiate purchase of intellectual property or, alternatively, may seek competitive bids in relation to elements of the proposal that are able to be tendered without encroaching on the property rights of the proponent.

In order to demonstrate the government's intention in this area, private sector consultants are generally appointed as independent process auditors.

Examples

Victoria can point to a diverse range of projects undertaken over the past five years, or currently under development, including:

Private financing structures in place

Eye and Ear Hospital Carpark -- A developer has provided a six level commercial carpark to meet hospital needs, on hospital property.

Co-generation Plants -- Construction of seven privately owned gas turbines on six hospital sites provides steam and electric power, with surplus electricity being sold into the State grid.

Yan Yean Water Treatment Plant -- A private consortium has constructed a plant and contracted to provide required quantities of water to defined quality standards.

Werribee Hospital -- A privately owned, 127 bed public hospital at Werribee, in one of Melbourne's urban growth corridors, is funded through the Victorian Accelerated Infrastructure Program.

Private investment in infrastructure projects being developed under the IIPV

Bulk Chemical Storage -- A Bulk Chemical Storage Facility is to be relocated from the Port of Melbourne. The Victorian Government has approved in principle an arrangement whereby port and road transport facilities are to be provided for use by the owner and clients of a private bulk chemical storage facility.

Public Transport Corporation Automated Ticketing -- A private consortium is to provide integrated revenue collection and ticketing services to the Public Transport Corporation for trams, trains and buses operating in the metropolitan public transport system.

Computer Aided Emergency Call Taking and Dispatch -- A private consortium will provide a computer aided call-taking and dispatch service to a group of Victorian emergency services organisations, including the Victoria Police Force the State Emergency Service and the Melbourne Ambulance Service.

Latrobe Regional Hospital-- It is intended that a private health provider will contract with Government to provide public hospital and ancillary services using, as a base for payment, the Government's hospital case mix funding structure. A Registration of Capability document was issued early in October 1995.

Nobbies -- Redevelopment of visitor facilities at a picturesque coastal location with a large colony of fur seals and adjacent to a popular penguin parade attraction.

Two major current projects, the Melbourne City Link and the New Prisons Project provide concrete examples of the effectiveness of the techniques and processes that have been adopted in Victoria. These two projects are dealt with in detail in following pages.

4.   The Melbourne City Link

The Melbourne City Link, being undertaken under the *Infrastructure Investment Policy for Victoria*, is part of a state government program of major projects designed to revitalise the state. The Victorian Government is currently negotiating with a private consortium, Transurban, to undertake the construction and operation of the two major bypass roads that will constitute the City Link, in the state capital of Melbourne.

The project has an estimated construction cost of more than A$ 1.2 billion and, together with financing and associated charges, is expected to total approximately A$ 1.7 billion. It will be one of the largest infrastructure projects ever undertaken in Australia.

Scope

Construction work will involve some 22 kilometres of road, tunnel and bridge works. Essentially, the project will link Melbourne's existing fragmented freeway system (see map on the following page).

The main components of the project are:

- the significant upgrading and widening of two of Melbourne's three existing major freeways, particularly the freeway to Melbourne's main airport where a peak period express lane will be provided to improve access by public transport;

- linking of the three major freeways;

- the building of a new 23.5 metre high bridge across the Yarra River with two 120 metre high towers. These towers will be as tall as the larger city buildings and will add a significant element to Melbourne's landscape;

- the construction of two tunnels under the Yarra River. One, at 3.4 km in length, will be one of the longest road tunnels in the world;

- a sculptured northern gateway, 60 metres long, with a "wall" of 58 coloured columns 30 metres high. The sculpture has been designed to give a positive first message, about the cultural values and commercial strengths of Victoria, to visitors arriving from the airport. It symbolises a modern technological city;

- substantial landscape improvements along the route, particularly improved facilities for cyclists and pedestrians, with the development of new pathways and the planting of over 2 000 trees; and

- a market potential to toll 300 000 vehicles per day at commencement of operation.

Purpose

The project is designed to:

- implement road infrastructure programs on a competitive market basis;

- assist greater competitiveness by Victorian industry through improved access between industry and the port, rail and airport facilities;

- reduce travel times significantly for motorists, especially during peak periods;

- reduce through traffic in the city centre, especially commercial vehicles on inner city streets;

- provide a high standard of access to the city centre and recent developments to the south of the Yarra River including a riverside retail, restaurant and entertainment development, a Casino, and an Exhibition Centre, and other major sporting and entertainment venues such as the Melbourne Cricket Ground and the Melbourne Arts Centre; and

- develop aesthetically pleasing and architecturally distinctive structures that enhance the appeal of the City of Melbourne.

Challenges

From the Victorian public point of view, the City Link marks an abrupt change to the way major urban roads are delivered and paid for. The Link, as a privately built, owned and operated road, stands in strong contrast to the surrounding myriad of roads, built and managed in the traditional way by the state.

From a project direction and project management point of view, the City Link posed a number of major challenges. These challenges were not so much of an engineering or planning nature (although in places these were quite significant, for example with the use of full electronic tolling) but rather they go to the core of the interface between the private and public sectors. The challenges were:

- negotiating an appropriate balance in the Concession Deed and related documents on the allocation of risk between the private consortium and public sector and at the same time allowing the project to be attractive enough to investors to raise through debt and equity approximately $1.7 billion;

- ensuring that legislation imposes the appropriate rights and obligations on the consortium as to the design, construction, tolling, operation and maintenance of the Link and defines the state's responsibilities to protect the public;

- developing a methodology for defining the Link within the broader state transport infrastructure system, whereby actions taken by either the consortium or the government are acknowledged in a debit/credit relationship;

- establishing a regime for dispute resolution between the state and the consortium; and

- in building a new way of conducting business with the private sector, ensuring that the specialist skills, technologies, financing techniques and etiquette learned are transferred to the wider public sector.

Structure

Consistent with the government's policy guidelines, the private sector bears the commercial risk for its part in the infrastructure project. Transurban is to assume responsibility for the financing and economic risks inherent in the design, construction and operation of the project for a concession period of between thirty and forty years. At the expiry of the concession period, the consortia will transfer the assets to the Government, at no cost and in a fully maintained state.

Transurban is expected to be floated next year as a major new Victorian-based public company. Its capitalisation on listing will see it marked as one of Victoria's top ten companies.

The project is proceeding on the basis of a revenue stream generated entirely by direct electronic tolling. The tolling system must satisfy the performance criteria of operating at freeway design speed and not slowing the flow of traffic.

There will be some state government funding for the project (approximately $247 million), but this will not be in the form of underwriting or providing a financial guarantee for any part of the City Link project. In the main, this will be used for property acquisition and works that the state has requested in conjunction with the project.

The role of the Victorian government in the project is to:

- facilitate the project with the establishment of necessary legislation that clearly defines the role of the government and the consortia;

- take responsibility for Planning Scheme Amendment processes, liaise with the Commonwealth government and ensure the project meets Australian Loan Council objectives;

- assist in the acquisition of required property;

- establish protocols concerning use and confidentiality of documents and information; and

- through the operation of the Melbourne City Link Authority, ensure that the project is undertaken in accordance with agreements and arrangements entered into between the consortium and the state.

Bidding

Private sector response to the offer by the State of Victoria for private involvement in the City Link project was highly successful. Two bidders invested in excess of $10 million each in endeavouring to win the mandate for the project. Hundreds of people were involved on each side for several months. All four of Australia's major banks and several offshore banks were fully committed to the bids. This response would not have happened if the political pedigree for the project was not correct, nor the infrastructure policy clear.

Success factors

In addition to the clear policy direction given by the government to the private sector in establishing the ground rules for projects of this type, there are a number of other factors which have contributed to the success of the undertaking of the City Link project. These are largely due to the way in which the project has been set up.

The Chief Executive Officer of the Melbourne City Link Authority has identified the following factors as key pre-conditions for the successful process that has been established and maintained for this landmark project:

- *the establishment of a dedicated task force at the outset.* An examination of the history of the project reveals that there has been a considerable gestation time and a great deal of ground work accomplished by the public sector. The setting up of a task force almost three years ago, formed the basis of the subsequent Melbourne City Link Authority, established in December 1994. That early group undertook important work on route options, financial analysis and financial options. It essentially enabled the public sector to establish a base of expertise;

- *early recruitment of key legal and financial consultants.* An early decision was taken to keep the City Link Authority as a small and flexible organisation made up of a group of permanent core staff and supplemented by outside expertise according to the developing needs of the project. In many ways the types of skills that the Authority brought in are not those that the public sector has traditionally provided. A project like the City Link requires commercial and financial skills typically found in the private sector;

- *creation of a Committee of the state government to oversee the project.* The Committee, chaired by the Victorian Premier, includes the Victorian Treasurer and the Ministers for Planning, Roads and Ports and Major Projects. This group brings together the key strategic portfolio areas and has enabled issues that might otherwise pose obstacles to progress to be dealt with. This group also brought to bear the political will necessary to drive the project;

- *appointment of experienced public sector officials to head and service the Authority, with secondees from key government departments such as Treasury and Finance, Planning, Roads Authority and Premiers.* In a similar way to its approach to acquiring private sector skills, the Authority identified key people in the public sector and brought them in. In one case, there is a reporting arrangement back to the secondee's department, the Department of Treasury and Finance. This arrangement has worked extremely well;

- *establishment of a private sector board of directors to oversee the Authority.* Members of the Board have eminent engineering, financial and legal backgrounds from the private sector, providing skills and a perspective that have made a central contribution to the course of the project and towards its private/public sector relationship;

- *drafting of key front end brief documents and template legal documents well in advance.* The recruitment of legal specialists enabled early preparation of necessary documents and positioned the Authority one step ahead of the consortia;

- *appointment of a Process Auditor to oversee the integrity of the assessment process of the private bids.* Right from the time that the Government decided to request detailed submissions from two consortia, it was essential to ensure that the selection process was handled with the utmost propriety. The bids involved considerable expenditure by both consortia. The appointment of an independent Process Auditor has made a significant contribution to achieving an integrity outcome; and

- *the maintenance of the highest levels of complete security and confidentiality of the bid assessment process, thereby preventing any subversion of the integrity of the process.* Throughout the selection process and subsequent negotiations with the successful consortium, the Authority has been under enormous scrutiny to maintain confidentiality.

5. Private prisons

Background

Existing situation

The Victorian prison system currently consists of 14 publicly owned and operated prisons spread across both metropolitan and non-metropolitan locations. The existing system has a number of inadequacies requiring high priority improvements. Among these are:

- *Antiquated facilities.* The building stock of the three prisons to be replaced is antiquated and obsolete, in some cases, over 100 years old;

- *Requirement for further improvement to work practices.* Prison operating costs are high, and despite recent improvements, public sector correctional services work practices have substantial scope for further efficiency gains; and

- *Projected growth in prisoner numbers.* The existing capacity of the Victorian prison system is inadequate (for example, Victoria's only maximum/medium security women's prison has a design capacity of 60 prisoners but currently accommodates on average over 90 prisoners).

The New Prisons Project

In December 1993, the Victorian Government announced the New Prisons Project ("NPP") to seek private sector involvement in the delivery of three new prisons in Victoria to replace three existing prisons. The NPP was established within the Department of Justice and expressions of interest were sought, through public advertisement, for private sector involvement in the financing, design, construction and management of the new prisons.

The prisons being developed under the NPP are:

- a 125-bed women's prison to be located in the State capital city, Melbourne (currently under construction);

- a 600-bed medium security men's prison to be located in rural Victoria; and

- a 600-bed multi-functional men's prison to be located in metropolitan Melbourne.

These facilities will accommodate over 60 per cent of female and approximately 50 per cent of male prisoners in Victoria.

Government objectives

The Government has agreed that the implementation of the NPP should achieve the following objectives:

- replace the existing inadequate and ageing plant with new facilities and increase the capacity of correctional facilities to meet projected demand;

- reduce the costs of infrastructure development;

- reduce the costs of correctional services via the adoption of improved work practices;

- ensure the scope and quality of services to prisoners is maintained and/or enhanced, without compromising security and safety;

- meet government policy objectives of private sector involvement in prison operations by introducing private equity into Victorian prison infrastructure, with consequential transfer of risk to the private sector;

- establish competition among private and public sector providers of correctional services;

- introduce new approaches to the design, construction and management of prisons.

Government approval process

The government will approve private sector participation in the NPP only where such involvement is clearly the best solution for the state. At the same time, the government is committed to minimising the cost of uncertainties faced by the private sector in pursuing project opportunities.

Consistent with the *Infrastructure Investment Policy for Victoria*, the government has approved implementation of the prisons project subject to the achievement of specified commercial arrangements and functional requirements. As a pre-requisite, the government will proceed with the letting of contracts only if bidders can demonstrate a net saving in the total cost per prisoner per year to government, including facilities and prison services, when compared to the total recurrent costs for the replaced prisons, adjusted for inflation. This will ensure the cost to government of the new prisons will be below existing recurrent costs of service delivery, and avoids the cost to government of delivering new buildings under traditional government approaches.

The NPP has encouraged the private sector to improve correctional services and management through the use of innovative and cost effective prison operation proposals. The Project Briefs for the prisons contain prison management, design and construction specifications based on outcome rather than prescriptive guidelines. These proposals, however, must achieve Victorian prison system imperatives by meeting legislative requirements, (which, inter alia, ensure that Government retains legal custody of prisoners), Victorian Government Corrections Policy objectives, and Australian and international correctional standards.

Prompt but staggered delivery

The NPP has developed an approach which staggers the start of the bidding process for the three prisons, and thereby:

- spearheads the Program by fast tracking the smallest, most achievable and most critical prison (the 125-bed women's prison) for completion by mid 1996;
- delivers the second (men's 600-bed medium security) prison by early 1997; and
- delivers the third (men's 600-bed multi-functional) prison by late 1997.

Key features of the Victorian approach to the NPP

The commercial arrangements adopted for the NPP represent a financial hybrid of the conventional Build Own Operate and an innovative partial equity approach. These arrangements were adopted to address government, Treasury and private sector requirements in relation to infrastructure privatisation.

The key features of this approach are:

- the Victorian government nominates preferred sites available to the consortia through sale or lease. Consortia are also able to put forward alternative sites;

- a detailed brief and draft contract documents are issued at the same time to bidders to avoid prolonged legal negotiations. The management requirements have been developed in output rather than prescriptive terms to encourage innovative proposals from the bidders;

- the successful consortium owns the new prison;

- government contracts with the owner, under a single Prison Services Agreement, to supply both facilities and services on the basis that the owner develops the prison, including commissioning, and is responsible for the maintenance and operation of the prison, including provision of services;

- the preferred position of the government is that the owner has an equity investment in the prison. The level of equity is nominated by the consortia as part of their bids. The return on equity investment to the owner is based on the performance of the operator in providing correctional services and programs;

- contract payments are broken into three parts covering the:

  - availability charge, which is the cost of provision of correctional facilities to a standard sufficient for prisoners to be accommodated and correctional services to be delivered to legislative and specified requirements;
  - correctional services fee, which is the cost of provision of corrective services, education, training, health and other programs; and
  - performance-linked fee, which gives a return on equity to the owner, provided that specified positive outcomes for both prison services and facilities are achieved (for example with respect to prison security, safety, health care programs);

- the government's position on risk allocation is to place with the consortia all risks for the design, construction, ownership and management of the prison. The government's position on risks acceptable to the government extends only to the allocation of prisoners within defined limitations and correctional policy changes;

- government safeguards to ensure that private operators deliver the best possible correction facilities include:

  - overall responsibility for prisoners including sentence planning, initial prisoner assessment and classification remains with the State;

  - day-to-day supervision is the responsibility of the contractor/manager under government supervision, subject to Victorian prison system standards;

  - the government retains the right to periodically re-tender the contract for correctional services, every three years after an initial five-year period.

- payment to the private operators is based on performance, dependent on the degree to which service delivery outcomes are achieved. The contract will not be renewed if the specified standards are not met;

- the government has clear step-in rights, if necessary to maintain required service levels;

- the government has unfettered access to all aspects of the operation of the prison and will extend an Official Visitors Program to the new prisons to allow a community overview; and

- requirements for public accountability through Freedom of Information legislation and a State Ombudsman have been extended to the private prisons.

- the creation of a competitive correctional services industry with regulation through an Office of Commissioner for both the public and private systems. This will require changes to the existing organisational structure; and

- an emphasis on probity both internally in tendering processes and externally among bidders. An independent probity auditor has been appointed to provide guidance on internal tendering processes and a probity investigation team comprehensively investigates all short-listed and preferred bidders.

Advantages of the Victorian approach

Attractiveness to the Victorian government

The NPP represents a private investment proposal of high attractiveness to the Victorian Government, because, consistent with the Infrastructure Investment Policy for Victoria:

- a high degree of private sector investment has been encouraged in the design, construction and management of correctional facilities and services previously exclusively provided by the public sector. This has been achieved with broad scope for innovation;

- the project has proven attractive for private sector investment which has extended to equity involvement by major Australian financial institutions;

- a low level of required government support, which is limited to facilitation including planning and other approval processes. No government guarantees have been given beyond a fee for service commitment under contractual arrangements;

- minimal government risk exposure. Design, construction, ownership and management risks are allocated to the private owner;

- the project has served to address a lack of understanding by the private sector of the level and nature of risk transfer required by government;

- high direct cost impact. The government receives new infrastructure and services for the same price as the total recurrent cost of the existing services that they are replacing; and

- achievement of broad Victorian Government objectives of reduction of the State's indebtedness and reduction in public employment.

Benefits to regional economies

It is apparent from the large amount of interest in siting the prisons, that many Local Councils and regional bodies have recognised the significant local employment and other economic benefits to Victorian communities from the prisons.

Benefits from introducing competition into the corrections industry

The exposure of the industry to private sector innovation should result in improved methods and new perspectives on prisoner management and design, leading to an overall better prison system in terms of training and industry experience and therefore, one would expect, better rehabilitation of prisoners.

Substantial improvement is already evident in the work practices of competing state-run prisons and a more positive culture is likely among all staff involved in corrections.

6. Key success factors

The failure or sub-optimum performance of various infrastructure investment projects can be attributed to a number of causes, prominent among which are:

– inadequate research;
– inadequate planning;
– inadequate resources; and
– insufficient government commitment.

Because these projects typically are complex and very often constitute a radical departure from the ways in which such projects have been delivered in the past, they demand project planning of a high order.

Among the aspects that require early and methodical planning are:

clear government acknowledgement. At the outset, the Government should clearly identify the strategic importance or desirability of a project;

adequate research. In order for projects to commence on an informed basis, it is essential that sufficient early research is conducted in the following areas:

 • financial feasibility;
 • technical feasibility; and
 • private sector market feasibility.

clear objectives. The project objectives should be to satisfy a particular need for services, defined in functional terms, not to provide a particular piece of infrastructure. Optimum benefits are to be achieved where private proponents are given maximum scope to devise innovative solutions to service needs;

specific government requirements. Project implementation is typically greatly assisted by the establishment and documentation of a clear set of government objectives or requirements from the project. These objectives should include the cost to government benchmark against which the decision to proceed will be made. Typically, objectives arise in the areas of risk transfer, introduction of investment funds or equity, establishment of structural precedents, establishment of a competitive market-place and the like;

adequate resources. The implementation process is resource intensive. Resources typically include Cabinet Committees, Steering Committees, Project Team and Directorate, and securing the appropriate legal, financial or technical advisers as required. It is particularly important to include private sector participation in the government decision making structure to ensure that the public sector requirements are balanced with the commercial imperatives as decisions are made;

government approval Strong government commitment to proceed is required before an approach to the market is made. This ensures that the project enjoys sufficient political and governmental support to sustain it during the difficulties typically experienced during major project implementation. These difficulties should not be underestimated. They are unique to the current circumstances where public providers are being restructured and a new public-private interface is being negotiated and defined;

fair dealings with the market. Government has an obligation to match the level of responsiveness that it requires from private sector consortia bidding for projects. Communications should be facilitated between the government, through the Project Team, and the various markets within which the project arises. A program of activities and milestones should be published and adhered to as far as possible;

reasonable shortlists. Given the resource intensity of the detailed submissions process, the number of shortlisted proponents generally should not exceed three;

published evaluation criteria. Detailed documentation requesting comprehensive submissions should include the evaluation criteria against which the financial, technical, operational, legal and other aspects of submissions will be evaluated;

high level probity. It is essential that the market is provided with a degree of comfort as to the probity with which confidential information is managed and that the consortia bidding for major projects are all dealt with equally;

other. Other success factors that appear to contribute to smooth project implementation include issuing draft legal documentation and requiring that proposed departures from these documents be identified in detailed submissions. Another factor that has arisen from time to time is to match the implementation process to the size, scope and sophistication of the market in selecting one-or two-stage implementation.

MAIN SALES OUTLETS OF OECD PUBLICATIONS
PRINCIPAUX POINTS DE VENTE DES PUBLICATIONS DE L'OCDE

AUSTRALIA – AUSTRALIE
D.A. Information Services
648 Whitehorse Road, P.O.B 163
Mitcham, Victoria 3132   Tel. (03) 9210.7777
    Fax: (03) 9210.7788

AUSTRIA – AUTRICHE
Gerold & Co.
Graben 31
Wien I   Tel. (0222) 533.50.14
    Fax: (0222) 512.47.31.29

BELGIUM – BELGIQUE
Jean De Lannoy
Avenue du Roi, Koningslaan 202
B-1060 Bruxelles   Tel. (02) 538.51.69/538.08.41
    Fax: (02) 538.08.41

CANADA
Renouf Publishing Company Ltd.
5369 Canotek Road
Unit 1
Ottawa, Ont. K1J 9J3   Tel. (613) 745.2665
    Fax: (613) 745.7660

Stores:
71 1/2 Sparks Street
Ottawa, Ont. K1P 5R1   Tel. (613) 238.8985
    Fax: (613) 238.6041

12 Adelaide Street West
Toronto, QN M5H 1L6   Tel. (416) 363.3171
    Fax: (416) 363.5963

Les Éditions La Liberté Inc.
3020 Chemin Sainte-Foy
Sainte-Foy, PQ G1X 3V6   Tel. (418) 658.3763
    Fax: (418) 658.3763

Federal Publications Inc.
165 University Avenue, Suite 701
Toronto, ON M5H 3B8   Tel. (416) 860.1611
    Fax: (416) 860.1608

Les Publications Fédérales
1185 Université
Montréal, QC H3B 3A7   Tel. (514) 954.1633
    Fax: (514) 954.1635

CHINA – CHINE
Book Dept., China National Publications
Import and Export Corporation (CNPIEC)
16 Gongti E. Road, Chaoyang District
Beijing 100020   Tel. (10) 6506-6688 Ext. 8402
    (10) 6506-3101

CHINESE TAIPEI – TAIPEI CHINOIS
Good Faith Worldwide Int'l. Co. Ltd.
9th Floor, No. 118, Sec. 2
Chung Hsiao E. Road
Taipei   Tel. (02) 391.7396/391.7397
    Fax: (02) 394.9176

CZECH REPUBLIC –
RÉPUBLIQUE TCHÈQUE
National Information Centre
NIS – prodejna
Konviktská 5
Praha 1 – 113 57   Tel. (02) 24.23.09.07
    Fax: (02) 24.22.94.33
E-mail: nkposp@dec.niz.cz
Internet: http://www.nis.cz

DENMARK – DANEMARK
Munksgaard Book and Subscription Service
35, Nørre Søgade, P.O. Box 2148
DK-1016 København K   Tel. (33) 12.85.70
    Fax: (33) 12.93.87

J. H. Schultz Information A/S,
Herstedvang 12,
DK – 2620 Albertslung   Tel. 43 63 23 00
    Fax: 43 63 19 69
Internet: s-info@inet.uni-c.dk

EGYPT – ÉGYPTE
The Middle East Observer
41 Sherif Street
Cairo   Tel. (2) 392.6919
    Fax: (2) 360.6804

FINLAND – FINLANDE
Akateeminen Kirjakauppa
Keskuskatu 1, P.O. Box 128
00100 Helsinki

Subscription Services/Agence d'abonnements :
P.O. Box 23
00100 Helsinki   Tel. (358) 9.121.4403
    Fax: (358) 9.121.4450

***FRANCE**
OECD/OCDE
Mail Orders/Commandes par correspondance :
2, rue André-Pascal
75775 Paris Cedex 16   Tel. 33 (0)1.45.24.82.00
    Fax: 33 (0)1.49.10.42.76
    Telex: 640048 OCDE
Internet: Compte.PUBSINQ@oecd.org

Orders via Minitel, France only/
Commandes par Minitel, France exclusivement :
36 15 OCDE

OECD Bookshop/Librairie de l'OCDE :
33, rue Octave-Feuillet
75016 Paris   Tel. 33 (0)1.45.24.81.81
    33 (0)1.45.24.81.67

Dawson
B.P. 40
91121 Palaiseau Cedex   Tel. 01.89.10.47.00
    Fax: 01.64.54.83.26

Documentation Française
29, quai Voltaire
75007 Paris   Tel. 01.40.15.70.00

Economica
49, rue Héricart
75015 Paris   Tel. 01.45.78.12.92
    Fax: 01.45.75.05.67

Gibert Jeune (Droit-Économie)
6, place Saint-Michel
75006 Paris   Tel. 01.43.25.91.19

Librairie du Commerce International
10, avenue d'Iéna
75016 Paris   Tel. 01.40.73.34.60

Librairie Dunod
Université Paris-Dauphine
Place du Maréchal-de-Lattre-de-Tassigny
75016 Paris   Tel. 01.44.05.40.13

Librairie Lavoisier
11, rue Lavoisier
75008 Paris   Tel. 01.42.65.39.95

Librairie des Sciences Politiques
30, rue Saint-Guillaume
75007 Paris   Tel. 01.45.48.36.02

P.U.F.
49, boulevard Saint-Michel
75005 Paris   Tel. 01.43.25.83.40

Librairie de l'Université
12a, rue Nazareth
13100 Aix-en-Provence   Tel. 04.42.26.18.08

Documentation Française
165, rue Garibaldi
69003 Lyon   Tel. 04.78.63.32.23

Librairie Decitre
29, place Bellecour
69002 Lyon   Tel. 04.72.40.54.54

Librairie Sauramps
Le Triangle
34967 Montpellier Cedex 2   Tel. 04.67.58.85.15
    Fax: 04.67.58.27.36

A la Sorbonne Actual
23, rue de l'Hôtel-des-Postes
06000 Nice   Tel. 04.93.13.77.75
    Fax: 04.93.80.75.69

GERMANY – ALLEMAGNE
OECD Bonn Centre
August-Bebel-Allee 6
D-53175 Bonn   Tel. (0228) 959.120
    Fax: (0228) 959.12.17

GREECE – GRÈCE
Librairie Kauffmann
Stadiou 28
10564 Athens   Tel. (01) 32.55.321
    Fax: (01) 32.30.320

HONG-KONG
Swindon Book Co. Ltd.
Astoria Bldg. 3F
34 Ashley Road, Tsimshatsui
Kowloon, Hong Kong   Tel. 2376.2062
    Fax: 2376.0685

HUNGARY – HONGRIE
Euro Info Service
Margitsziget, Európa Ház
1138 Budapest   Tel. (1) 111.60.61
    Fax: (1) 302.50.35
E-mail: euroinfo@mail.matav.hu
Internet: http://www.euroinfo.hu//index.html

ICELAND – ISLANDE
Mál og Menning
Laugavegi 18, Pósthólf 392
121 Reykjavik   Tel. (1) 552.4240
    Fax: (1) 562.3523

INDIA – INDE
Oxford Book and Stationery Co.
Scindia House
New Delhi 110001   Tel. (11) 331.5896/5308
    Fax: (11) 332.2639
E-mail: oxford.publ@axcess.net.in

17 Park Street
Calcutta 700016   Tel. 240832

INDONESIA – INDONÉSIE
Pdii-Lipi
P.O. Box 4298
Jakarta 12042   Tel. (21) 573.34.67
    Fax: (21) 573.34.67

IRELAND – IRLANDE
Government Supplies Agency
Publications Section
4/5 Harcourt Road
Dublin 2   Tel. 661.31.11
    Fax: 475.27.60

ISRAEL – ISRAËL
Praedicta
5 Shatner Street
P.O. Box 34030
Jerusalem 91430   Tel. (2) 652.84.90/1/2
    Fax: (2) 652.84.93

R.O.Y. International
P.O. Box 13056
Tel Aviv 61130   Tel. (3) 546 1423
    Fax: (3) 546 1442
E-mail: royil@netvision.net.il

Palestinian Authority/Middle East:
INDEX Information Services
P.O.B. 19502
Jerusalem   Tel. (2) 627.16.34
    Fax: (2) 627.12.19

ITALY – ITALIE
Libreria Commissionaria Sansoni
Via Duca di Calabria, 1/1
50125 Firenze   Tel. (055) 64.54.15
    Fax: (055) 64.12.57
E-mail: licosa@ftbcc.it

Via Bartolini 29
20155 Milano   Tel. (02) 36.50.83

Editrice e Libreria Herder
Piazza Montecitorio 120
00186 Roma   Tel. 679.46.28
    Fax: 678.47.51

Libreria Hoepli
Via Hoepli 5
20121 Milano   Tel. (02) 86.54.46
    Fax: (02) 805.28.86

Libreria Scientifica
Dott. Lucio de Biasio 'Aeiou'
Via Coronelli, 6
20146 Milano   Tel. (02) 48.95.45.52
          Fax: (02) 48.95.45.48

JAPAN – JAPON
OECD Tokyo Centre
Landic Akasaka Building
2-3-4 Akasaka, Minato-ku
Tokyo 107   Tel. (81.3) 3586.2016
          Fax: (81.3) 3584.7929

KOREA – CORÉE
Kyobo Book Centre Co. Ltd.
P.O. Box 1658, Kwang Hwa Moon
Seoul   Tel. 730.78.91
          Fax: 735.00.30

MALAYSIA – MALAISIE
University of Malaya Bookshop
University of Malaya
P.O. Box 1127, Jalan Pantai Baru
59700 Kuala Lumpur
Malaysia   Tel. 756.5000/756.5425
          Fax: 756.3246

MEXICO – MEXIQUE
OECD Mexico Centre
Edificio INFOTEC
Av. San Fernando no. 37
Col. Toriello Guerra
Tlalpan C.P. 14050
Mexico D.F.   Tel. (525) 528.10.38
          Fax: (525) 606.13.07
E-mail: ocde@rtn.net.mx

NETHERLANDS – PAYS-BAS
SDU Uitgeverij Plantijnstraat
Externe Fondsen
Postbus 20014
2500 EA's-Gravenhage   Tel. (070) 37.89.880
Voor bestellingen: Fax: (070) 34.75.778

Subscription Agency/   Agence d'abonnements :
SWETS & ZEITLINGER BV
Heereweg 347B
P.O. Box 830
2160 SZ Lisse   Tel. 252.435.111
          Fax: 252.415.888

**NEW ZEALAND –
NOUVELLE-ZÉLANDE**
GPLegislation Services
P.O. Box 12418
Thorndon, Wellington   Tel. (04) 496.5655
          Fax: (04) 496.5698

NORWAY – NORVÈGE
NIC INFO A/S
Ostensjoveien 18
P.O. Box 6512 Etterstad
0606 Oslo   Tel. (22) 97.45.00
          Fax: (22) 97.45.45

PAKISTAN
Mirza Book Agency
65 Shahrah Quaid-E-Azam
Lahore 54000   Tel. (42) 735.36.01
          Fax: (42) 576.37.14

PHILIPPINE – PHILIPPINES
International Booksource Center Inc.
Rm 179/920 Cityland 10 Condo Tower 2
HV dela Costa Ext cor Valero St.
Makati Metro Manila   Tel. (632) 817 9676
          Fax: (632) 817 1741

POLAND – POLOGNE
Ars Polona
00-950 Warszawa
Krakowskie Prezdmiescie 7 Tel. (22) 264760
          Fax: (22) 265334

PORTUGAL
Livraria Portugal
Rua do Carmo 70-74
Apart. 2681
1200 Lisboa   Tel. (01) 347.49.82/5
          Fax: (01) 347.02.64

SINGAPORE – SINGAPOUR
Ashgate Publishing
Asia Pacific Pte. Ltd
Golden Wheel Building, 04-03
41, Kallang Pudding Road
Singapore 349316   Tel. 741.5166
          Fax: 742.9356

SPAIN – ESPAGNE
Mundi-Prensa Libros S.A.
Castelló 37, Apartado 1223
Madrid 28001   Tel. (91) 431.33.99
          Fax: (91) 575.39.98
E-mail: mundiprensa@tsai.es
Internet: http://www.mundiprensa.es

Mundi-Prensa Barcelona
Consell de Cent No. 391
08009 – Barcelona   Tel. (93) 488.34.92
          Fax: (93) 487.76.59

Libreria de la Generalitat
Palau Moja
Rambla dels Estudis, 118
08002 – Barcelona
    (Suscripciones) Tel. (93) 318.80.12
    (Publicaciones) Tel. (93) 302.67.23
          Fax: (93) 412.18.54

SRI LANKA
Centre for Policy Research
c/o Colombo Agencies Ltd.
No. 300-304, Galle Road
Colombo 3   Tel. (1) 574240, 573551-2
        Fax: (1) 575394, 510711

SWEDEN – SUÈDE
CE Fritzes AB
S–106 47 Stockholm   Tel. (08) 690.90.90
          Fax: (08) 20.50.21

For electronic publications only/
Publications électroniques seulement
STATISTICS SWEDEN
Informationsservice
S–115 81 Stockholm   Tel. 8 783 5066
          Fax: 8 783 4045

Subscription Agency/Agence d'abonnements :
Wennergren-Williams Info AB
P.O. Box 1305
171 25 Solna   Tel. (08) 705.97.50
          Fax: (08) 27.00.71

Liber distribution
International organizations
Fagerstagatan 21
S-163 52 Spanga

SWITZERLAND – SUISSE
Maditec S.A. (Books and Periodicals/Livres
et périodiques)
Chemin des Palettes 4
Case postale 266
1020 Renens VD 1   Tel. (021) 635.08.65
          Fax: (021) 635.07.80

Librairie Payot S.A.
4, place Pépinet
CP 3212
1002 Lausanne   Tel. (021) 320.25.11
          Fax: (021) 320.25.14

Librairie Unilivres
6, rue de Candolle
1205 Genève   Tel. (022) 320.26.23
          Fax: (022) 329.73.18

Subscription Agency/Agence d'abonnements :
Dynapresse Marketing S.A.
38, avenue Vibert
1227 Carouge   Tel. (022) 308.08.70
          Fax: (022) 308.07.99

See also – Voir aussi :
OECD Bonn Centre
August-Bebel-Allee 6
D-53175 Bonn (Germany) Tel. (0228) 959.120
          Fax: (0228) 959.12.17

THAILAND – THAÏLANDE
Suksit Siam Co. Ltd.
113, 115 Fuang Nakhon Rd.
Opp. Wat Rajbopith
Bangkok 10200   Tel. (662) 225.9531/2
          Fax: (662) 222.5188

**TRINIDAD & TOBAGO, CARIBBEAN
TRINITÉ-ET-TOBAGO, CARAÏBES**
Systematics Studies Limited
9 Watts Street
Curepe
Trinidad & Tobago, W.I. Tel. (1809) 645.3475
          Fax: (1809) 662.5654
E-mail: tobe@trinidad.net

TUNISIA – TUNISIE
Grande Librairie Spécialisée
Fendri Ali
Avenue Haffouz Imm El-Intilaka
Bloc B 1 Sfax 3000   Tel. (216-4) 296 855
          Fax: (216-4) 298.270

TURKEY – TURQUIE
Kültür Yayinlari Is-Türk Ltd.
Atatürk Bulvari No. 191/Kat 13
06684 Kavaklidere/Ankara
      Tel. (312) 428.11.40 Ext. 2458
        Fax : (312) 417.24.90
Dolmabahce Cad. No. 29
Besiktas/Istanbul   Tel. (212) 260 7188

UNITED KINGDOM – ROYAUME-UNI
The Stationery Office Ltd.
Postal orders only:
P.O. Box 276, London SW8 5DT
Gen. enquiries   Tel. (171) 873 0011
          Fax: (171) 873 8463

The Stationery Office Ltd.
Postal orders only:
49 High Holborn, London WC1V 6HB
Branches at: Belfast, Birmingham, Bristol,
Edinburgh, Manchester

UNITED STATES – ÉTATS-UNIS
OECD Washington Center
2001 L Street N.W., Suite 650
Washington, D.C. 20036-4922 Tel. (202) 785.6323
          Fax: (202) 785.0350
Internet: washcont@oecd.org

Subscriptions to OECD periodicals may also be
placed through main subscription agencies.

Les abonnements aux publications périodiques de
l'OCDE peuvent être souscrits auprès des
principales agences d'abonnement.

Orders and inquiries from countries where Distribu-
tors have not yet been appointed should be sent to:
OECD Publications, 2, rue André-Pascal, 75775
Paris Cedex 16, France.

Les commandes provenant de pays où l'OCDE n'a
pas encore désigné de distributeur peuvent être
adressées aux Éditions de l'OCDE, 2, rue André-
Pascal, 75775 Paris Cedex 16, France.

12-1996

OECD PUBLICATIONS, 2, rue André-Pascal, 75775 PARIS CEDEX 16
PRINTED IN FRANCE
(14 97 02 1 P) ISBN 92-64-15417-5 – No. 49294 1997